WITHDRAWN

"WHAT PEOPLE CALL PESSIMISM"

Studies in Austrian Literature, Culture, and Thought

"WHAT PEOPLE CALL PESSIMISM":

Sigmund Freud, Arthur Schnitzler, and Nineteenth-Century Controversy at the University of Vienna Medical School

by

Mark Luprecht

Ariadne Press

Library of Congress Cataloging-in-Publication Data

Luprecht, Mark.
  "What people call pessimism": Sigmund Freud, Arthur Schnitzler, and nineteenth-century controversy at the University of Vienna Medical School / Mark Luprecht.
      p. cm. --(Studies in Austrian literature, culture, and thought)
    Includes bibliographical references and indexes.
    ISBN 0-929497-11-2. -- ISBN 0-929497-28-7 (pbk.) .
    1. Schnitzler, Arthur, 1862-1931--Knowledge--Medicine. 2. Freud, Sigmund, 1856-1939--Influence. 3. Pessimism in literature.
  4. Universität Wien. Medizinische Fakultät--Influence. 5. Vienna (Austria)--Intellectual life. I. Title. II. Series.
  PT2638.N5Z834 1990
  833'.8--dc20   90-761
                                                                   CIP

Cover design by George McGinnes

Copyright © 1991
by Ariadne Press
270 Goins Court
Riverside, California

DEDICATION

To my father, Erich Luprecht (1916–1989), whose golden Viennese heart continues to beat, and to my mother Ruth, who shared that heart for a lifetime.

ACKNOWLEDGMENTS

My sincere thanks are directed to the Fulbright Commission for a study grant which allowed me to pursue research in Vienna during the 1985–1986 academic year. The Austrian-American Educational Commisission: Dr. Günther Frühwirth, Mrs. Eva Schussek, and Mr. Fassl, helped in many ways to make the year fruitful and rewarding. In Vienna, the editor of Arthur Schnitzler's letters and diaries, Peter Michael Braunwarth, of the Österreichische Akademie der Wissenschaften, was particularly kind and helpful as was the entire staff at the University of Vienna Institut für Geschichte der Medizin.

To Dr. Audrey Wilson, who was supportive throughout the conception and execution of this work, and who gave generously of her limited time, unique talent, and cheerful spirit, I owe an especial note of gratitude. She has been the embodiment of a friend's friend.

"WHAT PEOPLE CALL PESSIMISM"

Table of Contents

INTRODUCTION

A letter from Sigmund Freud to Arthur Schnitzler has received a good deal of recent attention and acted as the instigation for the following study. The psychiatrist, writing to congratulate the playwright on his sixtieth birthday (May 15, 1922), made "a confession which for my sake I must ask you to keep to yourself." He had avoided Schnitzler, he wrote, "from a kind of aversion to meeting my double" (H. Schnitzler, "Briefe" 96). As Kupper and Rollman-Branch have established, a large number of biographical similarities existed between the two, among them: religion, professional training, and geographical location (111–113), but Freud drew attention to broader affinities, to Schnitzler's "presuppositions, interests, and conclusions," which he considered identical to his own. The psychoanalyst felt a philosophical kinship with the poet:

> Your determinism as well as your skepticism – what people call pessimism – your preoccupation with the truths of the unconscious and of the instinctual drives in man, your dissection of the cultural conventions of our society, the dwelling of your thoughts on the polarity of love and death; all this moves me with an uncanny feeling of familiarity. (E. Freud 339)

1

The purpose of this work is to determine the accuracy of Freud's perception, especially concerning the three "-isms" mentioned in the quotation. An attempt is further made to find the extent to which both men's world-views were affected by their shared experience at the University of Vienna Medical School. In his essay of 1955, "Hofmannsthal und seine Zeit," Hermann Broch argued that Vienna around the year 1880 was the site of a "gay apocalypse." An almost complete absence of values (*Wert-Vakuum*) obtained but could be disregarded because of accomplishments by institutions such as the medical school of the University of Vienna, which had risen to prominence in the course of a century (76–77). Both Freud and Schnitzler were closely bound with the medical school at the time of which Broch wrote. Freud had received his medical degree in March 1881, while Schnitzler had begun his medical training in the fall of 1879.

Yet Broch failed to note that the medical school was itself a philosophical battleground just prior to Freud's and Schnitzler's matriculation, a fact which helps to explain Freud's assertion that both Schnitzler and he shared a skeptical and even a pessimistic outlook. Erna Lesky, in *The Vienna Medical School in the Nineteenth Century* (1976), has given the broad outlines of the struggle among various schools of thought, among them therapeutic skepticism and nihilism, whose proponents argued for the primacy of diagnosis over treatment, and therapeutic optimism, which posited cure as the physician's primary duty (118ff). Whether or not William M. Johnston is correct in suggesting that therapeutic nihilism remained "a major trend in Viennese thought long after it had waned at the Medical Faculty" (71), the conflict between passive diagnosis and active intervention in medicine and the philosophical underpinnings of these conflicting views must have influenced medical students such as Freud and Schnitzler and contributed in shaping their perspectives.

A second major nonmedical dialogue also must have had an impact on the outlooks of medical students. At about the same time as the Second Viennese Medical School was being established around the tenets of therapeutic skepticism, in the late 1840s, a debate concerning the validity of the materialistic world-view began. Deeply involved in the controversy was a prominent instructor of both Freud and Schnitzler, the physiologist Ernst von Brücke. Both the therapeutic debate and the broader questions raised by materialism lingered at the University of Vienna Medical School throughout the nineteenth century.

Prior to examining the two controversies, the study begins with a brief history of the First Viennese Medical School, followed by a discussion of the pathologist, Karl von Rokitansky (1804–1878), founder of the Second Viennese Medical School, and the therapeutic notions upon which the school was based. Though a recent (1979) biography of Rokitansky by Robert Miciotto focused belated attention on a significant figure in intellectual history, Miciotto inexplicably omitted any discussion of Rokitansky's nonmedical essays. Rokitansky and the diagnostician Josef Skoda (1805–1881) were the main proponents of therapeutic skepticism, which opposed medical intervention based upon abstract conceptualizations of disease, followed by, from a twentieth-century viewpoint, barbaric remedies (Lesky, "Rokitansky" 38–41; Sternberg 40–41). This reluctance to treat patients prior to a definitive diagnosis led to extreme statements, like the following by Skoda's disciple, Joseph Dietl (1804–1878): "While the old school carried on therapy before engaging in research, the new school began researching in order to be able to understand therapy . . . Our strength lies in knowledge, not in action . . ." (Lesky, *School* 122).

Beyond depicting the change in medical philosophy represented by the skepticism of Rokitansky and Skoda as well as the rise of therapeutic optimism in its wake, a discussion of Rokitansky's nonmedical work lends further depth to this intellectual backdrop of Schnitzler's and Freud's medical education. Rokitansky, as is shown by an examination of his autobiography (1877) and his essays, "Der selbstständige Werth des Wissens" (1867) and "Die Solidarität alles Thierlebens" (1869), founded his world-view upon Charles Darwin's theory of evolution as well as Arthur Schopenhauer's idealism and pessimism.

There follows a discussion of the impact of these skeptics'

ideas and of the debate concerning materialism upon two of Freud's and Schnitzler's mutual instructors, Brücke and the psychiatrist Theodor Meynert (1833–1892), as well as that of the therapeutic optimism of Johann von Oppolzer (1808–1871). Both Meynert and Brücke had broad interests and wrote on diverse topics: a volume of Meynert's poetry was published posthumously in 1906, while Brücke penned a number of works bearing on aesthetics, most notably *Schönheit und Fehler der menschlichen Gestalt* (1891).

It is both fitting and structurally expedient to link Freud's contention of a shared determinism and skepticism with Schnitzler to the two debates at the medical school. Determinism, "the doctrine that human action is not free . . . that everything that happens is determined by a necessary chain of causation" (*Oxford Universal Dictionary* 1: 494), is correlated to the controversy surrounding therapy, that is, concerning the ability and responsibility of medicine to aid the patient. The second shared perspective cited by Freud, skepticism, is associated in this study with the materialist debate at the medical school. Skepticism, whether "the opinion that real knowledge of any kind is unattainable," or merely "doubt as to the truth of some assertion or supposed fact," is commonly held in opposition to religion, as one of its early definitions evidences (*OUD* 2: 1803). The lines separating these "-isms" get blurred: determinism and materialism frequently go hand-in-hand, and therapeutic skepticism is after all a form of skepticism. Thus the distinctions drawn are hardly inflexible, nor need they be, and serve mainly organizational purposes.

Before looking closely at Schnitzler's oeuvre, a brief examination will be made in Chapter Two of Freud's relationship to the University of Vienna Medical School, to medicine in general, and to his own manifestations of those factors he felt Schnitzler shared. Relatively little need be said concerning Freud's determinism: psychoanalytical method and theory have quite often been correlated to the influence of Freud's materialist medical educators, most substantially by Peter Amacher in *Freud's Neurological Education and Its Influence on Psychoanalytic Theory* (1965). Less explored is the effect of determinismson Freud's theory of civilization and his world-view in general, though there is ample evidence, both in Ernest Jones' biography, *Sigmund Freud, Life and Work*, and Freud's autobiographical sketch, *Selbstdarstellung*, that the father of psychoanalysis was greatly impressed by both Brücke and Meynert and might well have been influenced by them in his nonmedical thoughts and attitudes (Jones 1: 40, 72; Freud, *Autobiographical Study* 8–9). Other authors have alluded to the likelihood that Freud's medical education had a broad influence. William Johnston wrote that "it was from medical teachers rather than from philosophers or literati that Freud imbibed the attitudes that enabled him to inaugurate psychoanalysis" (229). And, at the conclusion of his study, Amacher commented that "[i]t is unlikely that Freud was influenced by the ideas of his teachers in these early but crucial theories, and not in the wider development of psychoanalysis" (84).

An integral part of Freud's theory of civilization was played by religion. The psychoanalyst's position concerning religion and civilization formed the core of most of his late work. *Totem and Taboo, The Future of an Illusion, Civilization and Its Discontents, Moses and Monotheism* and the previously mentioned autobiographical sketch serve as the primary texts, with reference being made to *The Ego and the Id, Beyond the Pleasure Principle*, "The Question of Lay-Analysis," *Group Psychology and the Analysis of the Ego* and *History of the Psychoanalytic Movement*. The fact that Freud turned to nonmedical topics in his later years requires some discussion in itself. Bruno Bettelheim, in *Freud and Man's Soul* (1982), argued that Freud had been consciously mistranslated in an attempt to make of psychoanalysis an exact science, a contention Freud himself did not entertain.

Though hardly as influential in intellectual history as Freud's, Schnitzler's work seemed to Freud to support his speculations, and can be viewed, to the extent Freud's interpretation is valid, as plausible substantiation for the influence of the medical faculty's nonmedical thought. With the exception of Michael Worbs, who in his 1983 study *Nervenkunst*, devoted three pages (196–198) to the subject, Schnitzler's intellectual relationship with the medical school has not been explored. Perhaps this neglect is due to the author's making light of his medical education in his autobiography, *Jugend in Wien* (99, 187). Nevertheless, the years spent at medical school must have had a great impact on one who said, "whoever has been a medical man can never stop being one, for medicine is a world-view" (O. Schnitzler, 53). An important role in both men's world-views was played by the "Jewish question," though neither Freud nor Schnitzler was an observing Jew. Neither man developed either a very complete theory or response to the phenomenon, but there is ample evidence of strong personal affects and responses in both cases. Three works of Schnitzler are of particular significance in assessing his philosophical posture: the novel, *Der Weg ins Freie;* the comedy, *Professor Bernhardi;* and Schnitzler's autobiography, all of which examine the contemporary situation of Jews in Austria.

These works and a number of creations of the 1920s are considered in Chapter Three, in order to develop a composite of Schnitzler's relation to the perspectives of determinism and skepticism. As in the case of Freud, Schnitzler's creativity was channeled in a somewhat different direction in his last years. Though known primarily as a dramatist, the writer turned increasingly to fiction and aphoristic expression in his last decade. Whether or not William H. Rey's thesis, that this late prose is the peak of Schnitzler's achievement, is correct (Rey, *Prosa*), for the purpose of this study its use is appropriate for two reasons: first, the prose works approximate in time the greater part of Freud's nonmedical production, and second, they are characteristic of Schnitzler's thematic concerns in general and can represent the whole of his work (*Prosa* 12).

Beyond a close consideration of some of Schnitzler's late fiction: "Flucht in die Finsternis," "Traumnovelle," and *Therese,* use is made of the author's novelty, *Der Geist im Wort und der Geist in der Tat: Vorläufige Bemerkungen zu zwei Diagrammen,* in which Schnitzler developed a typology of human activity and spirit. Of great significance, too, is the volume entitled *Aphorismen und Betrachtungen,* which contains the essence of Schnitzler's own opinions about a variety of topics, and a notebook of reflections entitled "Über Psychoanalyse." Finally, Schnitzler's diaries, especially those still unpublished – from his youth – are thoroughly examined. These uncensored and spontaneous documents, maintained from 1879 to 1931, are essential to the enterprise of ascertaining the author's actual personal thoughts and opinions. According to Otto P. Schinnerer, Schnitzler "did not consider it impossible that it [his diary] might someday be considered more valuable than his work," and stored the notebooks in a bank vault (Lindken 522). Such direct inroads into Schnitzler's thinking are necessary. Rey's point in this regard is well-taken; Schnitzler concealed a great deal of profundity in his work, and one cannot say in his case that the work is the man (*Prosa* 13).

No attempt is made to pass aesthetic judgments or to evaluate the validity of psychoanalytic theory or of Freud's anthropological speculation. Rather, both Freud and Schnitzler are approached from a cultural-historical perspective, that is, as products and producers of a given culture. Themes in their works are interpreted, juxtaposed, and shown as plausibly evolving from their medical forebears. Though the emphasis of this study is upon assessing the extent of truth in Freud's estimation of the similarity of Schnitzler's ideas with his own (page 1, above), providing the intellectual climate of their medical school education sheds light upon their respective contributions. A fourth section, or conclusion, summarizes the evidence culled from the interpretation of the late works of both authors. The study concludes with a brief comparison of those aspects of their *Weltanschauung* relating to the nonmedical debates at the University of Vienna Medical School in the nineteenth century.

The result of this comparison of Freud's and Schnitzler's underlying perspectives, with each other, and as they evolved from views circulating at the University of Vienna Medical School, provides a useful addition to the ever-increasing discussion of fin-de-siècle Vienna's part in shaping a twentieth-century consciousness. That the city had a role in this creation, or at least in the recognition and analysis of the new consciousness, has long been noted, from Stefan Zweig's *Die Welt von Gestern* (1944), to Carl E. Schorske's *Fin-de-Siècle Vienna* (1980). Following Philip Rieff, in *Freud: The Mind of the Moralist* (1961), Schorske argued that a new consciousness, a "psychological man," emerged from the Vienna of Freud and Schnitzler (Rieff 361–394; Schorske 3–23). This study focuses on significant ideological facets of the two men's intellectual world, which, if Schorske is correct, play an important part in the way we perceive ourselves. To what extent did Freud and Schnitzler converge in their *Weltanschauungen*? And to what degree were their attitudes and views derived from the nonscientific intellectual currents of their medical training? The answers to these questions will give proper due to an inadequately explored source of twentieth-century thought: the philosophical foundations and controversies of the Second Viennese Medical School.

Note on Translations. I have translated all citations from documents of the University of Vienna Medical School, Schnitzler's works, and all secondary materials. In the event of ambiguous terms, I have included the German word, sometimes with an alternative translation in parentheses. Quotations from Freud's work are taken from the English translations noted in the Bibliography. I have, however, made one substitution. The German *"Trieb,"* usually rendered "instinct," has been altered, for reasons given by Bruno Bettelheim (103–107), to his suggestion, "impulse." Bettelheim's argument about other mistranslations is compelling, but usage has so accustomed the ear and mind to phrases such as "ego," "super-ego," and "id," that "I," "super-I," and "it," are jarring to the point of distraction.

CHAPTER ONE

Historical Background:
The Second Viennese Medical School

Two fundamental disagreements which existed within the medical faculty of the University of Vienna during the nineteenth century were of particular importance in the world-views of Sigmund Freud and Arthur Schnitzler. The first was concerned with the possibilities of therapy, and with the responsibility of the physician. The Second Viennese Medical School was founded upon the work of pathologist Karl von Rokitansky and internist Josef Skoda, both of whom were skeptical as to the possibility of healing patients with the therapy at hand. Their position, as Heinrich Buess has maintained, must be interpreted against the backdrop of the very low standard of therapy that obtained in the first half of the century (Buess 304–305). That this inherently medical consideration might have had extensive nonmedical influence was suggested by William M. Johnston (71).

A second controversy of a more general philosophical bent began at about the same time, focusing, in Vienna, around the figures of physiologist Ernst von Brücke and anatomist Josef Hyrtl. Beyond possessing strong and very different personalities, these

9

physicians came to represent antithetical *Weltanschauungen.* Support of broad concepts such as materialism, anti-vitalism, and political and social freedoms was attributed to Brücke and his adherents, while Hyrtl and his followers advocated traditional positions, whether scientific or sociopolitical. Thus, the Hyrtl School argued for the existence of a "life-force" (*Lebenskraft*), posited the insufficiency of materialism, and fostered state tutelage (Rothschuh 88–90).

The polarities wrought by these two controversies at the medical school are perceptible in the works of both Freud and Schnitzler. The ways in which these men responded to the intellectual climate created by such basic disagreement help explain similarities and differences in their world-views.

To present a balanced picture of the intellectual environment of the medical school, one must be aware of the origins of the so-called Second Viennese Medical School. There had been a medical faculty at the University since its inception in 1365, but, as the historian Josef von Aschbach wrote, "it was not much of a medical school during the first 400 years of its existence" (Vogl 283). Reasons for the mediocrity of the school stemmed first from the low standards of medical practice in general and the "paralyzing effect of Scholasticism on all learning" in the later middle ages, and then from the ubiquitous apathy of the "war-torn and plague-ridden Vienna" of the sixteenth and seventeenth centuries (Vogl 283).

Maria Theresa's appointment of Gerard Van Swieten as "pro-medicus" in charge of medical education in Austria in the mid-eighteenth century put an end to the medical faculty's stagnancy. Van Swieten, who came to Vienna in the summer of 1745, created the first teaching hospital, and by eliminating the influence of the College of Jesuits made possible systematic instruction in anatomy through the use of regular dissections (Vogl 286–287). The so-called First Viennese Medical School, which arose around Van Swieten's reforms, flourished for about sixty years.

This "exciting era . . . was followed by an abrupt decline, not due to any lack of men of ability but solely because of the oppressive political atmosphere that had settled upon Vienna and Austria" (Vogl 290). Medicine in the early nineteenth century, like cultural life in Austria in general, found change and foreign influence repellent (Neuburger 41). The Biedermeier period found its expression, insofar as the Viennese medical faculty was concerned, in the virtual dictatorship of Baron Joseph Andreas Stifft, the "archreactionary" court physician who removed almost all the most promising of the school's leaders and replaced them with "politically trustworthy nonentities" (Vogl 290). Perhaps "nonentities" is too neutral a description of physicians who, according to Buess, were deeply mistrusted for their greed and corruption, and who themselves laughed with scorn at those unfortunates who actually trusted them (306).

Medical care during the first three decades of the nineteenth century was, as Buess vividly showed, at a very low point indeed. Two distinct but related factors were involved in this nadir of Austrian history, elements that went deeper than the corruption of individual physicians, or the nepotism and intellectual incest fostered by Baron Stifft (Neuburger 48). Therapeutic practices, and the philosophical foundation behind these practices constituted the enemy against which the ranks of the Second Viennese Medical School allied themselves.

Underlying medical theory during the so-called *Vormärz* were the tenets of Friedrich Wilhelm von Schelling's *Naturphilosophie.* This philosophy posited the unity and rationality of the "All," as well as the identity of nature and spirit, both in the realm of the Macrocosm (the *Allnatur*) and in the microcosm of the human being. The task of the natural philosopher, according to Schelling, was to seek the polarity operating throughout nature. In medical theory a dualistic approach to the human body, known in German as *Solidarpathologie,* extended back to late antiquity. In this view the body was held to be a "passive, sluggish mass" consisting of dull or overexcited fibers (Buess 305).

More important for medical theory than any of Schelling's precepts was the entire enterprise of basing a physical science upon abstract notions concerning the constitution of the body. Erna

Lesky referred to medical practice during the early nineteenth century as operating in a "natural-philosophical dream" (*School* 107), and Max Neuburger pointed to the absurdity of trusting absolutely a philosophy that thought to cure illness and solve the problems of living through "fanciful ideas" and "bombastic phrases" which, without the corrective of experience, led to indulgence (*Entwicklung* 37).

Attempting to explain life or disease on the basis of opposites or dualisms without recourse to, or concern for, a science based upon observation or experience can be, as it was in early nineteenth-century medicine, extremely brutal and even dangerous. In the dogma of *Solidarpathologie*, stimulation (*Reiz*) of the area of the symptom would lead to cure. As Buess noted, even eclectic physicians such as Christoph Wilhelm Hufeland (1762–1836) viewed blood-letting, emetics, and opium as the three heroes of medicine. Buess cited medical historian J. J. Petersen, who was only possibly exaggerating when he commented that more people died of the forceful remedies of the Scots empiricist John Brown (1735–1788) than in the French Revolution (Buess 306).

This, then, is the background against which the presuppositions of therapeutic skepticism and nihilism of the Second Viennese Medical School must be judged. One finds censorship accompanied by intellectual stagnation. Theory was elevated at the expense of praxis, from which sometimes brutal, often apathetic, medical therapy sprang. Finally, greed and corruption were prominent in a profession populated by cynics.

Two men were at the center of the new faculty and new philosophy of therapy at the University of Vienna: Karl von Rokitansky and Josef Skoda. With one important and inexplicable exception, namely the opinion of the eminent German biologist and philosopher, Ernst Haeckel, the accomplishments of the new school were unanimously applauded.

The "miracle" of the Second Viennese Medical School, arising from a "political and scientific wilderness" (Vogl 290), began to take form in 1832 with the appointment of Rokitansky as "Prosektor" at the General Hospital in Vienna. The twenty-seven-year-old had not had an easy youth, as his autobiography makes evident. Rokitansky's *Lebenserinnerungen* (1878) is itself an example of the attempt at absolute objectivity that was the hallmark of Rokitansky's and Skoda's medical method.

An example of Rokitansky's clinical detachment can be seen in the description of a delicate aspect of his father's character. "I believe he was a man with a very animated sex-drive," Rokitansky wrote. "With his erudition and ambition, he could only infrequently be with his wife (where, for this reason, he found little kindness, and had to renounce satisfaction" (5–6). The author included, for thoroughness no doubt and without any question of its interest to the reader, a list of organizations of which he was a member, honors he was awarded, and a register of sicknesses to which he fell a victim.

Yet, businesslike, cool, and thorough assessments are not to be equated with the inability to be emotionally affected. His father's grisly death in 1813, when Rokitansky was only eight, left an indelible impression on him: so horrible was the pain that the patient attempted to extract his own teeth. And the death in 1864 of the pathologist's sister, Therese, in an insane asylum, "placed me for a long time in a condition of inexpressible grief" (7, 12).

Experiences like these, a "basic melancholic disposition," and the "deep pessimism of his nature" (Lesky, *School* 107), engendered in Rokitansky an attraction to the philosophy of Arthur Schopenhauer. Early in his autobiography he wrote of the enterprise of narrating one's life as being itself a manly decision, "as I believe, with Schopenhauer, that there is no one who could decide to start his life over again." With a sentiment reminiscent of Schopenhauer's pessimism at its most extreme, Rokitansky summarized his life: "when I survey my life, which contrary to my previous expectation has lasted so long, I can say that it was, with few pauses, uninterrupted suffering of body and soul . . ." (12).

Rokitansky's fundamental pessimism was graphically portrayed in a lecture delivered before the Imperial Academy of Sciences on May 31, 1869, entitled, "The Solidarity of All Animal Life." In this essay the pathologist developed the thesis of the primal, even cellular, origin of suffering. Beginning with protoplasm and continuing throughout the evolutionary ladder, Rokitansky saw two primal phenomena (*Urphänomena*): hunger and movement. These forces comprised the possibility of an organism's existence, growth, diverse form, and manifold differentiation (4). Simultaneously, however, at all levels of organic sophistication, these same motivating factors, hunger and motility, created conflicting aims among organisms. Their satisfaction required aggressive behavior: in fact, Rokitansky stated, "the character of animals is aggressive, is aggression: from self-acting primal animals (*Urthiere*) to the organisms clearly conscious of their own aggression" (21). Werner Leibbrand in his essay "Karl von Rokitansky und Schopenhauer" accurately summarized the pathologist's extension of these thoughts in the societal sphere. Rokitansky, he wrote, "found [this aggression] reflected in mankind's interstate and governmental arrangements ('the battle for existence')" (77).

An individual's freedom was, for Rokitansky, a manifestation of his intellect, which, in his scheme, was constantly battling the human "character." This latter facet was the domain of aggression. In animals and barbarous humans, character had mastery over intellect. Education and civilization were assigned the task of channeling aggression into new streams, of finding "other, nobler motifs for character" (23). Despite the great importance of this task, Rokitansky reminded his audience, the basic aggressive nature of the human being, the "egoism" that required release from the body, had found more easily controlled outlets, but had not been exterminated or even diminished in strength. "Yet," the pathologist asked, "how often this [redirection] failed to succeed: how many fled openly into barbarism, and how many others wore the mask of civilization but lived in abstruse concealment from it? " (24).

Given clear checks upon animals' true characters, Rokitansky concluded, it was "clear and natural" that suffering could be the only result. Suffering was without question the lot of the animal kingdom, especially in the world of human beings – much more so, Rokitansky remarked, than was happiness. Indeed, joy was "actually only a gratified wish, an allayed suffering . . ." (24–25). Just as character (i.e., aggression), so suffering could assume several forms, and could have its direction altered by intelligence and civilization. Nevertheless, all animal life suffered: suffering was the link among animals, the solidarity to which the title of Rokitansky's essay referred (27). And, as with aggression, suffering could not be limited by civilization or intellect.

Some alleviation from suffering could be achieved through compassion. The German word *"Mitleid,"* literally, "suffering with," admirably suited Rokitansky's conception. Our suffering could be diminished only by our ability to transcend egoism and join in the suffering of others or an other. In Rokitansky's words this "noteworthy phenomenon," compassion, allowed the "individualized appearance" to be touched by the suffering of others, to suffer along and thus to mitigate one's own sorrow. As this paraphrase indicates, Rokitansky was influenced not only by Schopenhauer's pessimism, but also by his philosophic idealism. Thus the individual was the *"individualisierte Erscheinung,"* the individualized appearance. And, ultimately, the responsibility for our suffering was due to the world of appearances: one assumes, to our inability to fathom the noumenal (27). Compassion was, perhaps, an inroad into the other.

Still more pronounced was the influence of idealistic philosophy in Rokitansky's 1867 lecture, "The Independent Value of Knowledge," also delivered to the Imperial Academy on May 31. Rokitansky began the talk by stating his theme: that knowledge, *per se,* was one of life's highest values (4–5). His approach, he continued, would be materialistic, though he was not a materialist, which was to say, he would argue his case from an organic, physiological point of view (5–6).

Rokitansky's position regarding materialism as a world-view had been stated in the Introduction to his *Handbook of General Pathological Anatomy* of 1846. As this *Weltanschauung* became the center of another great intellectual controversy in the Second Viennese Medical School, as will be seen, it is relevant to mention Rokitansky's stance as the founder of the school. Though there is no record of his involvement in a debate on the matter, he was affected by materialistic thought, insofar as it constituted an alternative to an abstract medicine based upon *Naturphilosophie.* In his Introduction he wrote: "A correct view of force and matter teaches that there is no force without a material foundation. Every phenomenon is the manifestation of a certain force or of combined forces, and these themselves are the outcome of certain conditions passing into others . . . the nature of the forces' original beings [was] slowly or quickly changing matter. Thus, every phenomenon is conditioned by matter" (Neuburger, "Rokitansky" 2). At the same time, however, Rokitansky asserted that life could not be reduced to the view that existence was a mere expression of a particular form or mixture of forms of matter coming into appearance (Neuburger, "Rokitansky" 3). As Neuburger stressed, Rokitansky steered the middle course: rejecting vitalism as well as a purely materialistic point of view (3). His position as an antivitalist, struggling against a speculative medicine based upon *Naturphilosophie,* led him, according to Lesky, to emphasize objectivity ("Carl von Rokitansky" 41).

The lecture of May 31, 1867, however, developed as an apologia of idealistic philosophy from the vantage point of natural science. Cognition and knowledge were accomplishments (*Leistungen*) of the personality (8). Indeed, Rokitansky proceeded, "the perceptible world surrounding us was essentially a creation of our personality." Objects attained a size and power as a result of the functions of our organs (11). Knowledge, for the pathologist, as Leibbrand noted, could not be separated from a knower. It was concerned with the reception and processing of sensate data (*Sinnendinge*) into perceptions (*Anschauungen*) (76).

All descriptions, classifications, inductions, and deductions, that is, the natural sciences, were based upon these perceptions. Simultaneously, perceptual knowledge was the basis of an idealistic world-view, for what was that complex of subjective, organic functions other than a series of *a priori,* subjective conditions under which perception was formed? (Leibbrand 36). Thus, Rokitansky could conclude, the world of representations (*Vorstellungswelt*) was just as real as the "world of realism," for the objects of the latter were just as dependent upon our perceptions as are our ideas ("Werth" 31). And the pathologist ended his lecture by reasserting our inability to know the noumena, while being certain that all things have "something" which was not perceptible but was nevertheless "the real" (38).

More significant for the medical school than Rokitansky's preference for Schopenhauer over Schelling was his native pessimism. For, unlike his predecessors, Rokitansky did not attempt to integrate his philosophical inclinations with his therapeutic methodology. His pessimism may have evolved from, or led to, his skeptical approach to therapy.

It would be inaccurate, in fact, to imagine Rokitansky's philosophical outlook as representing an abrupt departure from that of his predecessors of the First Viennese Medical School. Rather, as both his biographer, Robert Miciotto, and Erna Lesky have written, the pathologist's notions of therapy were partly in line with Schelling's *Naturphilosophie,* insofar as he stressed that the body (read "nature") could play a large role in its own cure (Miciotto 184; Lesky, "Ursprünge" 7). Maria Dorer interpreted Rokitansky's true goal as having been the establishment of a middle position between natural-philosophical speculation and pure empiricism (115). Rokitansky's medical methodology was rigidly empirical in its orientation and represented a clean break from the medical practices based upon abstract considerations.

Early in his career, Rokitansky wrote in his autobiography, he became convinced that autopsies could provide a mine of new or hitherto neglected information for the diagnostician. The pathologist set himself two tasks: "First . . . sorting the facts scientifically on a purely anatomical basis and thereby creating the subject of general pathological anatomy which would justify its separate existence as such . . . [and] second, demonstrating the applicability of the facts and their utilization for diagnosis in live patients" (Lesky, *School* 107). The striking originality of Rokitansky's method is lost today, but the pathologist had laid the foundation and created the material basis for the concept of "disease process." Symptoms had meaning and were no longer mere accidents, just as disease was no longer merely the interplay of polar forces, as it had been for the natural philosophers (*School* 108). Before, "in the era of *Naturphilosophie,* one could not ask about anything as prosaic as the seat of the illness, it was much cleverer to speculate about the force.... that secret something..." (Lesky, "Carl von Rokitansky" 40).

As was clear from Rokitansky's two-part methodology, facts were given preeminence in diagnosis. Disease could be understood only through the investigation of the disease site, and though dynamic forces might exist, they were irrelevant to the acquisition of knowledge of disease because of their inaccessibility through observation (Miciotto 72).

The pathologist was unique even in simple terms of the numbers of cases handled. The medical historian Max Neuburger reports that Rokitansky performed some two thousand autopsies per year during his stint at the General Hospital in Vienna (*Entwicklung* 53). Corresponding to the second of Rokitansky's professional aims, autopsy findings were, without exception, dictated into a report. A visiting student of Rokitansky's in 1847, Adolf Kussmaul, wrote that these reports were "uncommonly instructive. They related the essentials of the findings in such compressed brevity and yet so exhaustively . . . that I immediately began to copy them" (*Jugenderinnerungen* 284).

Unfortunately, Rokitansky's lectures were far less impressive and helpful. The dispassionate attitude so useful to the objective ends of the scientist was less likely to stimulate an audience of medical students. The pathologist had the annoying habit of beginning every lecture with, "we recently left off . . .", including his first lecture of the semester (Benedikt 64). Kussmaul noted that Rokitansky's facial characteristics carried the stamp of great kindheartedness and reliability, though when autopsies revealed something unexpected, he could become quite animated (285). The description of Rokitansky, given by Henry Ingersoll Bowditch in 1859, captured the more usual countenance of the pathologist: "He has the true working head of a German—a more learned head than any I have seen—a head to be looked at; a massive skull with a quiet, dull eye, but indicating solid strength of intellect" (Johnston 225).

When one considers that Rokitansky had set as a goal the use of information gained from autopsies in the treatment of his patients, it is hardly surprising that an alliance was forged between the pathologist and his contemporary, the diagnostician Josef Skoda. Indeed, a student of the two, Moritz Benedikt, himself a teacher of Arthur Schnitzler, wrote that "the two men are not to be thought of as separate. Skoda was conjointly the reformer of therapy" (68). Therapeutic skepticism, as, indeed, therapeutic nihilism, is a conception most often associated with Skoda, though the latter term more accurately describes the views of Skoda's disciples. Unlike Rokitansky, Skoda left behind few nonmedical writings. But his philosophical stance, judging from the abstract of his medical faculty inaugural address of October 15, 1846, was virtually identical with the pathologist's. He, too, had his foundations in an idealistic materialism. While disallowing the tenets of vitalism, Skoda continued by noting that "there is no way to thoroughly explore the inner causes of phenomena, and it is childish to want to find them by means of arbitrarily admitted powers" (Sternberg 57). Skoda also recognized the limitations of science. "Medicine," he said, "like all empirical science, will never develop into a total and closed system" (Sternberg 57–58). Similar to Rokitansky, Skoda accepted part of the teaching of *Naturphilosophie,* seeing in nature the source of healing. In a book concerning typhoid fever, co-authored with Emil Dobler, were expressed the tasks of the physician according to Skoda. These included "the ascertainment of changes occurring in all organs of the body from the beginning to the end of the illness" (Sternberg 22). Skoda further insisted on taking into account "the curative means used by nature as well as the means that experience has so far indicated to be the most suitable for assisting nature in its activity" (Lesky, *School* 123). Nature was to be assisted by means proven effective empirically, a policy, as Maximilian Sternberg wrote, which showed the distance between Skoda and the practices of the natural-philosophical faculty of the 1830s (22).

With Skoda as with Rokitansky the emphasis of medical procedure, in this case diagnosis, was upon the factual or objective. During a controversy in 1831 as to the contagiousness of cholera, Skoda decided that direct observation was necessary: he personally traveled to Bohemia, where an epidemic was raging (Lesky, "Skoda" 2). Skoda revivified the use of auscultation and percussion techniques in making his diagnoses. Such direct methods stood in marked contrast to the practices of contemporary diagnosticians who had an "ontological conception" of the nature of disease and were concerned with classification (Sternberg 40).

Skoda introduced a tripartite methodology for diagnosis. He began with an examination to determine, on the basis of deviation from the norm of acoustical signs, possible physical changes in the organs. Next, any gross anatomical changes were ascertained: these were the bases of physical changes. This step required the observation of all organs possibly involved in the illness. Step three was the diagnosis: the cause of anatomical change. This required a consideration of all possible diseases causing the observed alterations. Diagnoses that involved illnesses with symptoms not perceived were excluded. The residue was the disease that explained the greatest number of symptoms (Sternberg 42–43). Skoda's method became known as the "diagnosis of exclusion" and represented, according to Erna Lesky, "a completely new way of thinking" (*School* 119). Sternberg did not consider the system new, but opined that Skoda had systematically developed the procedure into a rigorous principle (43).

Skoda's relations with Rokitansky were not based merely on philosophical kinship or upon their mutual insistence on empirical medicine. Rather, Skoda appreciated and employed Rokitansky's willingness to share the findings of his postmortem examinations. Use of Rokitansky's meticulously kept records became part of Skoda's painstaking procedure. Lesky observed that "in order to establish a single fact with certainty he compared in every case numerous observations in healthy and in sick people with the results of autopsies" (*School* 119). By checking "his physical findings with the aid of his friend and mentor Rokitansky at the autopsy table," Alfred Vogl related, Skoda "was able to develop a new clinical system of the pathology of the heart and lungs" (291).

Further, Skoda carried out serial tests with patients as part of his attempt to find the best treatment for various diseases. He also aided in the discontinuation of already "obsolete means" of therapy, such as blood-letting, while "preparations such as chloral hydrate and salicylic acid were taken up, and old proven means such as digitalis [and] quinine . . . were reexamined critically as to their effects . . ." (Lesky, *School* 123).

Skoda's approach to therapy must be viewed, similar to that of Rokitansky, as a response to the abstractions and excesses of his contemporaries. By all accounts he was a moderate man of few words and deliberate opinion (Buess 311). Unlike many of his predecessors and peers, Skoda was both aware of the gaps in medical knowledge and willing to admit them: "we are not in a position to know, understand, or explain," was a phrase that occurred in almost all his propositions, according to Benedikt (68). From a perusal of Skoda's pupils' notebooks, Max Neuburger concluded that the diagnostician must have been a fine teacher as well. From the pages of these collections: "there arose an abundance of knowledge and experience, the crystal-clear thought process of a diagnostician of exceptional precision, a keenness of criticism combined with a total candor concerning the limits of medical capability . . ." (*Entwicklung* 73). The cautious attitude of Rokitansky and Skoda and their insistence on empirical evidence prior to the implementation of therapy was merely an expression of skepticism at then-current medical practice.

The two skeptics were, for all their cool detachment, not devoid of compassion for their patients and not rigidly opposed to all intervention. Lesky described an episode in which Skoda was reprimanded by the directing council for performing a tracheotomy on a choking victim. And one of Skoda's lasting accomplishments was his discovery of the correct way to administer digitalis ("Josef Skoda" 2, 5).

In what became a *cause célèbre,* both Rokitansky and Skoda came to the defense of their colleague, Ignaz Semmelweis. This

Hungarian obstetrician noted that by having medical personnel scrub with soap and water, and by soaking their hands in chlorinated lime solution, the 18% obstetrical death rate was lowered to 1.2%. "When he reported his result to the Medical Society of Vienna, his paper was greeted with virulent attacks" (Lyons and Petrucelli 553). Indeed, a year later, in 1848, Semmelweiss, despite the intervention of Rokitansky and Skoda, was demoted. Whether or not this can be termed "Vienna's most notorious case of therapeutic nihilism," as Johnston maintained (226), the leaders of the "Second School" favored Semmelweis' new method, founded, as it was, upon statistical evidence.

The skepticism and practices of the new school encountered the resistance of the established faculty from the very beginning (Rokitansky, *Lebenserinnerungen* 30). The great German scientist, Hermann Helmholtz, described a typical objection to Skoda's technique of percussion and auscultation: "This was a gross-mechanical means of examination, of which an enlightened physician had no need. And one degraded the patient who was, after all, a human being, and disgraced him, as if he were a machine" (Sternberg 30).

More incriminating and simultaneously less comprehensible was the acerbic criticism leveled at the University of Vienna medical faculty by the famous German biologist Ernst Haeckel. Haeckel spent the summer semester of 1857 at Vienna; a letter to his parents written during that stint has recently been published. Haeckel was most damning of Rokitansky, who, he wrote, "appears totally apathetic toward science, as even he himself must recognize. At least, he pursues pathological anatomy with an indifference that is incomprehensible" (Haeckel 130). Equally surprising was Haeckel's critique of Rokitansky's postmortem method, or, rather, lack thereof. Indeed, what Haeckel observed was actually "butchery" (131). All organs, he observed, were offhandedly dissected, without an *in situ* examination. Then, after a cursory glance, a judgment was passed. Everything was done so hastily that almost every autopsy was completed within fifteen minutes or a half-hour (130).

Skoda fared a little better in Haeckel's evaluation. He lacked a sure and practical method, as well as humaneness and gentility. In their place he assumed the "stringent, elevated tone of a scholar" (134). The objections of the twenty-three-year-old visitor were not corroborated by other eyewitness accounts. It is possible that Rokitansky, after more than a quarter century of autopsies, found the work routine. And the number of postmortems undertaken would require speed. Both the seeming lack of interest and the rapidity which appeared to border on carelessness must have been particularly distressing to someone who was unaccustomed to work in a mortuary.

With the exception of physiologist Ernst von Brücke, Haeckel was rather irked by the entire medical faculty of 1857, each member of which held himself to be "the only one of his type; infallible and irreplaceable" (129). There was no disagreement, however, concerning the tremendous impact of Rokitansky and Skoda on the world of medicine. Kussmaul wrote that the influence upon his students of such a clear-thinking and intrepid head as Skoda's was enormous (292). Nor would Haeckel have gainsaid Benedikt's sweeping evaluation of Rokitansky's significance: "the entire medical world," he submitted, "belongs to Rokitansky's students" (66). After all, we must assume that Haeckel traveled to Vienna precisely on account of its reputation.

Nevertheless, therapeutic skepticism had a very short history. In his memoirs Rokitansky noted with disappointment that he had been mistaken in believing that the next generation would bring him a greater income through lecture and demonstration invitations (*Lebenserinnerungen* 30). Quite possibly the extremism of some of Skoda's disciples catalyzed the reaction against the therapeutic notions of the founders of the Second School. Certainly the statement of Josef Dietl, cited in the Introduction, was provocative.

Skoda himself was extremely cautious in his use of medications, using only those of whose effect and effectiveness he was certain (Buess 311). Kussmaul held that "the step from fundamental skepticism to nihilism was not large," and that both teacher and students forgot the actual task of medicine: healing. "It came to the point," Kussmaul wrote, "where certain young physicians were almost more curious concerning the confirmation of their diagnoses than with the process of cure" (293, 295).

But both Max Neuburger (*Entwicklung* 74) and Erna Lesky were opposed to such a negative assessment of the Rokitansky/ Skoda legacy. One observes, Lesky opined that "the much-scorned therapeutic nihilism signified not only the declaration of bankruptcy of the old *materia medica,* but also signified an acknowledgment of a new, rationally founded pharmacology" ("Ursprüngen" 7). Lesky insisted that Rokitansky and Skoda be termed skeptics and not be identified with their extreme disciples ("Ursprüngen" 2). In fact, as Lesky pointed out in another article, Skoda's medical stance included to a significant degree the teaching of preventive medicine, as evidenced by his defense of Semmelweis and his advocacy of hygienic-prophylactic measures to prevent cholera and typhus ("Pathology" 2).

Already by the 1860s the pendulum of medical philosophy was swinging away from the groundbreaking theory and practice of Rokitansky and Skoda and from the excesses of their students. Reform passed quickly into moderation: the "medical 'Sturm und Drang' period," as Buess named it, was over (312). The work of the founders of the Second Viennese Medical School was criticized mainly on two grounds: for its lack of concern for the patient and its disregard of the benefits philosophy had to offer. The critics, however, did not attempt to eliminate the new objectivity introduced by Skoda and Rokitansky.

The first-cited and more significant critique of therapeutic skepticism was championed by Johann von Oppolzer, a student of Skoda. When, at Easter 1850, a second medical clinic was opened in Vienna, Oppolzer was called from Prague to head it. Though recommended by his former teacher, Oppolzer had been chosen by ministers and not by the faculty. According to Benedikt, the ministers recognized that Skoda could educate thinking physicians but was not the man to foster practicing physicians (95). For this purpose Oppolzer was selected to fill a gap left by his former teacher.

Oppolzer received a cool reception from Rokitansky and

Skoda upon his arrival, owing both to the method of his appointment and to his medical philosophy of therapeutic optimism. "Healing," he noted, "is the ultimate aim of all medical research" (Lesky, *School* 126). Yet, elements of his training with Skoda remained. Helmut Leitner remarked that Skoda's influence was evident in Oppolzer's insistence that "the diagnosis must above all be an anatomical one" (Leitner, 5). At the same time, in contradistinction to the practice in Vienna, Oppolzer valued physiology more highly than pathological anatomy (Leitner, 5). Oppolzer's orientation, that of viewing disease from the vantage-point of physiological disturbance, "led logically," according to Vogl, "toward active and individualizing therapy, while at Skoda's clinic the guiding principle was still . . . to refrain from any action that might interfere with the natural healing power of the human organism" (293).

Significant, too, in the training of physicians was Oppolzer's attitude toward the patient, engendered by the stress he laid upon the role of physician as healer. One of his students, for whom Oppolzer's clinic was the "favorite station," Moritz Benedikt, noted the internist's skill at spontaneous diagnoses and continued: "He was enormously rich in therapeutic remedies. His conduct and the timbre of his voice displayed the greatest sympathy. The entire science of medicine did not possess a sedative with which the presence and consolation of Oppolzer at the patient's bedside could not compete" (75). The famous surgeon, Theodor Billroth, observed that one admired Skoda in his lonely greatness but quickly came to love Oppolzer (Neuburger, *Entwicklung* 75). When all therapy and medicine failed, wrote Lesky, the therapeutic optimist "knew how to talk the miserable person out of his or her despair and did not turn away . . ." (*School* 126).

Oppolzer, like Skoda, left little in writing. However, his address, "Über Lehr- und Lernfreiheit," delivered in 1861, exemplified his view of science and medicine. Sentiments similar to Skoda's and Rokitansky's could be perceived here: "True science," Oppolzer said, "is modest; it recognizes its limits." The representatives of science were constantly aware of what could not be done or known, and "practice resignation concerning where their science ends." That end-point, the limits of exact knowledge, was, as Rokitansky also knew, the limits of knowledge of the physical or material world (Oppolzer 5). Perhaps the most important view shared by Oppolzer and the skeptics was also expressed in his 1861 address: "The natural scientist bases his judgment in the last instance upon physical observation and healthy thinking. In this way he advances his knowledge of natural laws" (6). Therapy was to be based on observation which was also the path to a fuller recognition of the workings of nature.

Nevertheless, Oppolzer possessed an idealism lacking in his skeptical peers. True science, he maintained in the same speech, sought only to advance the good and beautiful; the goal of science was the ennoblement of humanity (5, 8). Part of the doctor's duty, as seen by Oppolzer, must have met with Skoda's approbation. That physician was best "for whom the spirit of science has become clear, who is educated through and through both spiritually and morally, and who through sharp judgment and thorough examination can quickly recognize the disease process . . ." (9). The rest of Oppolzer's prescription was doubtless less important to Skoda: "to heal, to alleviate, to console, and to perform without regard to self" (9). Also distant from the skeptic's program was Oppolzer's premise that philosophy should be studied along with the sciences in order that one might learn principles (10).

The pediatrician L. M. Politzer shared Oppolzer's sentiments. Five years after Oppolzer's address Politzer pulled away from the teachings of therapeutic skepticism in stating that "we are . . . herewith openly joining the ranks of those who believe that the purpose of a physician is to cure and to help, and that within the limits of present knowledge . . . it is his duty to make the widest use of active and . . . radical treatments . . ." (Lesky, *School* 146). This statement is in direct contrast to the extreme sentiments expressed by Dietl cited in the Introduction, above. Nor were Dietl's sentiments isolated. Johnston related the following eyewitness's anecdote concerning Vienna's General Hospital, dating as late as 1898: "A doctor who visited the hospital told me he saw a party of students sounding a woman who was dying of pleurisy or pneumonia, in order that they might each hear the crepitation in her lungs as her last moments approached. She expired before they left the ward. He said something about treatment in another case to the professor who was lecturing these young men. The professor's reply was 'Treatment, treatment, that is nothing; it is the diagnosis that we want'" (228). One observes that beyond a mere difference in points of view, between the belief that help was possible with existing therapy and medications and its opposite, there was a truly profound rift in Viennese medicine between those who viewed the physician primarily as a practitioner, and those who saw the doctor as a scientist. The difference between therapeutic skepticism/ nihilism and therapeutic optimism can be viewed in part as an argument over the priority of theory over praxis.

The unwillingness to abandon philosophical underpinnings was a source of further reaction against therapeutic skepticism. A major spokesman for retaining the structure offered to medicine by philosophy was Ernst von Feuchtersleben (1806–1849). This psychologist-psychiatrist was immersed in the issue of mind-body dualism, and in the plausibility of psychosomatic illness.

Spurred by "the Romantic totality desire," Feuchtersleben warned the Viennese against both an exclusively analytical approach to medicine (Lesky, *School* 153–154) and against over-specialization (Johnston 226). In his best-known work, *Zur Diätetik der Seele* (1838), he described the possibilities of self-healing through self-mastery. In this suggestion there was a hint of the skeptic's belief in the body's own ability to cure.

Feuchtersleben argued that medicine had need for a "philosophy which would fulfill the task of 'constantly following and regulating all the different trends, limiting, connecting, correcting and reconciling them within the idea of a higher unity'. . ." (Lesky, *School* 154). Which particular philosophy Feuchtersleben might have had in mind was not clear; his expectations were obviously high. Neither Rokitansky nor Skoda would have expended much effort in the search, that much is certain. One must note, however, that unlike predecessors of the Second Viennese School even a staunch defender of philosophy in medicine like Feuchtersleben was arguing for philosophy on the basis of its regulatory function and not as a constitutive principle. The skeptics had clearly made some strides.

The influence of the reforms of Rokitansky and Skoda can also be seen in the orientation of the Second Viennese School toward anatomy: knowledge of disease was to be based upon the results of postmortem examinations, upon observation of the changes wrought by disease. But, Erna Lesky wrote, by the 1870s the theory of disease had become more sophisticated. With the search for that uncanny being which caused disease, bacteria, a new field of research came to the fore. There followed an ever-increasing use of endoscope, microscope, and scalpel to advance deeper into the interior of the human body (Lesky, "Wien," 152). The need for microscopic investigation was met by physiologist Ernst Wilhelm von Brücke, by all accounts one of the most impressive members of the faculty.

This polymath was called to Vienna in 1849, where "he created the necessary balance against the then prevalent anatomical orientation of the . . . Medical School" (Vogl 294). Beyond an excellent training in medicine Brücke was fluent in Italian, French, and English and had attended lectures dealing with philosophy and logic, Greek tragedy, and Goethe and Schiller. He dabbled in poetry: his biographer-grandson Ernst Theodor, has included one effort which reflects the influence of German romanticism. In *Die Physiologie der Farben für die Zwecke der Kunstgewerbe* (1866) Brücke discussed a theory of color. Ten years earlier he had developed a phonetic alphabet. Finally, toward the end of his life, the physiologist turned to the problem of child care and safety in *Wie behütet man Leben und Gesundheit seiner Kinder* (1892).

Above all, Brücke was a highly accomplished painter, and, indeed, considered attempting an artistic career (E. T. Brücke 9). His concern for the visual arts was evidenced by two theoretical volumes written in his leisure-time: *Bruchstücke aus der Theorie der bildenden Künste* (1877), and *Schönheit und Fehler der menschlichen Gestalt* (1891).

In these volumes Brücke evinced a love for classical art and a nostalgia for luminaries of the Italian Renaissance: "Leonardo had at his disposal the entire treasury of the knowledge of his time . . . Today such knowledge is impossible . . . The contemporary artist could certainly make do even with the knowledge of Leonardo, indeed even with less, *if he were animated with the spirit of the old masters,* and possessed their artistic knowledge . . ." (*Bruchstücke* viii). I have emphasized a portion of the above quotation because it implied a romantic attitude, a certain wonder at the ultimate inscrutability of artistic creation. This stance would be paradoxical in the materialist world-view attributed to Brücke, but its presence was perceived by his grandson. After noting that Brücke approached a painting or sculpture not only with his aesthetic sensibility but also with the eyes of a precise researcher, the biographer related his grandfather's concession of art's transcendence (E. T. Brücke 137, 159). This served as an example for his grandson of the occasional and "delightful inconsistency" between Brücke's theoretical positions and his practice (156).

In his book of 1891 Brücke began by again expressing regret for the decline in artistic ability, by which, as becomes evident, he meant the deviation from classical aesthetic ideals (*Schönheit* 1). He idolized Michelangelo Buonarotti, who understood better than anyone "how to bring forth wonderful and harmonious effects from figures that were, of themselves, not above reproach," through his placement of the figures and his understanding of "line" (5). Following a discussion of the four factors involved in human beauty: skeleton, muscle, fat, and skin, Brücke summarized the fundamental aesthetic thesis of his work: that art should portray the most beautiful, "that which, in all positions and from all views provides the best lines." He argued, finally, that his conception of the beautiful was the universal (common) conception, traceable to artists of classical antiquity, to the Praxitelean period at which time it had passed into the general consciousness (*Schönheit* 151).

An analogous lack of respect for change was displayed by Brücke in political matters. A German Protestant anti-clerical, the physiologist did not employ the title granted him in 1872, though he sat in the aristocratic Austrian *Herrenhaus* after 1879 (Johnston 230–231). To the events of 1848 he stood, according to his grandson, "as later in his life, as objectively as possible vis-à-vis the events." Although he never joined a political party, his positions were consistently anti-reactionary, and thus approximated those of the Democrats (30).

Above all, in questions political, Brücke was an empiricist. On February 20, 1883 he argued against the establishment of confessional schools. "I understand little of politics," he said, ". . . so I have abstracted the rule from history, that it was never to a State's advantage to have mixed in religious affairs" (E. T. Brücke 126). Beyond this practical reason for keeping the Church out of schools, Brücke noted the spirit of understanding created by interdenominational schools (E. T. Brücke 127).

Brücke's avoidance of extreme positions separated him politically from his very close friend and fellow-scientist, Emil du Bois-Reymond (1818–1896). This schoolmate's "warlike atheism in his early years, or his passionate indictment of the French in 1870, were especially marked in contrast to the measured expression of Brücke, who nevertheless experienced events no less deeply" (H. Brücke xxvii). In debating with Du Bois over socialism, Brücke used the same nondogmatic approach apparent in his argument against confessional schools. He saw socialism as lacking insight into what motivated both humans and industry (H. Brücke 7). Later (July 15, 1848) he wrote his friend that, as opposed to Du Bois' view that the regulation of relations between capitalists and workers was the answer to the "social question": "I am of the opinion that such endeavors can lead to nothing, for this path will never lead to an accord between the real value of labor represented by the average worker and the price of his customary provisions" (H. Brücke 9).

Brücke's approach to problems, which his grandson described as critical rather than intuitive (124–125), was reflected in his demeanor. Moritz Benedikt found the physiologist something of an oddity in Vienna, with his red hair and fixed visage (60). A man who worked closely with him, Sigmund Exner, never saw Brücke laugh or even smile. Thus Brücke garnered a reputation for lacking

Gemütlichkeit, and for housing a "cold soul" (Benedikt 60–61). This dubious distinction was reinforced by Brücke's behavior at examinations. If a single question he posed were answered incorrectly he would be silent for the remainder of the session and would adamantly refuse to pass the candidate (Benedikt 61). Less well-known but equally important in understanding the man, as his grandson noted, were Brücke's love of the Austrian landscape, his constant yearning for the beauty of Italian art and the simplicity of its people, and his concern for the young (123).

However superficially unattractive Brücke's personality may have been, he commanded virtually universal respect. His lectures, according to Benedikt, were difficult and exceeded the audience's level of comprehension, particularly in physics (61). Yet Brücke's fellow-German, Ernst Haeckel, rated the physiologist as the foremost member of the University of Vienna medical faculty (136), despite Haeckel's opposition, enunciated in 1899, to the materialist world-view of Du Bois-Reymond (Husteda 421). In Brücke's laboratory, Erna Lesky wrote, students "learned not only physiology, but a new way of medical thinking" (*School* 228).

The new mode of thought that dominated Brücke's physiology laboratory originated in his own education under Johannes Müller (1801–1856) in Berlin. This embryologist "had inculcated a conviction that empirical physiology must vanquish romantic medicine" (Johnston 229–230). Disease and all bodily functions could and must be understood in terms of physical-chemical forces. Besides Brücke and Du Bois-Reymond, Hermann Helmholtz was also Müller's student, and those who devoted "all of their research and theories, as students and later . . . toward explaining the function of the organism in physical terms" became known as members of the "Helmholtz School" (Amacher 10).

Erna Lesky has cited a passage of Du Bois-Reymond which captured the essence of the Helmholtz School, including its fervor: "Brücke and I have conspired to spread the truth that no other forces are effective in the organism but the ordinary physical-chemical ones; wherever these have hitherto proved insufficient as an explanation, the physical-mathematical method should be used in concrete cases either to establish the manner of their effectiveness, or new forces should be postulated which would be of the same order as the physical-chemical ones and inherent in the substance, and hence would derive solely either from repulsive or from attractive components" (*School* 229). Brücke's work was centered on the revelation of these physical-chemical forces. His method of learning about the functions of an organism was to study "the forces inherent in matter" (*School* 235).

Ernest Jones, Sigmund Freud's biographer, summarized Brücke's view of physiology, as expressed in the Introduction to the textbook he authored: "Physiology is the science of organisms as such. Organisms differ from dead material in action — machines — in possessing the faculty of assimilation, but they are all phenomena of the physical world; systems of atoms, moved by forces, according to the principle of the conservation of energy . . . Progress in knowledge reduces [the forces] to two — attraction and repulsion. All this applies as well to the organism man" (1, 45–46). In this approach there was a continuation of the rejection of *Naturphilosophie* and Romanticism in medicine begun by the skeptics. Rokitansky, in his lecture "Die Solidarität alles Thierlebens," also reduced all organic activity to two causes, hunger and motility (4). As in Rokitansky's thought, Jones noted in Brücke's physiology an "evolutionary orientation . . . part of the general trend of Western Civilization" (1, 46–47).

Another close connection with the founders of the Second Viennese School can be perceived in what George Rosen wrote of the students of Johannes Müller: "the goal of medical science was to achieve an understanding of pathological processes for clinical application . . . In principle there was no essential difference between physiology and pathology . . ." (24). There was only a shift in emphasis from the use of anatomy to that of physiology as the means for uncovering the truth about disease and bodily functions. Rosen, in a statement as true of Rokitansky as it was of Brücke, defined the physiologist "and his friends [as] members of a generation of young physicians who insisted that medical problems receive scientific treatment based more on laboratory experiment and less on clinical observation" (27). The scale seemed again to be tipping in favor of theory versus praxis, as it had under the therapeutic skeptics.

Like Skoda and Rokitansky, Brücke did not view his scientific-medical method as simply the most logical. For, as Adam Brücke stated, "It had an ethical dimension: the ethos of truthfulness, of intellectual sincerity, of respect for reality – a reality inaccessible to the dialectic arts but without which there was no truth" (xxiv). We will meet with these sentiments again in discussing Freud's conception of a *Weltanschauung*. And Siegfried Bernfeld, in "Freud's Earliest Theories and the School of Helmholtz" implied a further similarity shared by Brücke and his student in their approach to science. For the physiologist, as for Freud, "science mattered more than . . . death . . . scientific work merge[d] with life into one steady stream of activity" (352).

Despite the obvious integrity of his position, Brücke met with opposition, both for his materialist philosophy as well as his experimental technique. Leading the anti-materialist forces in Viennese medicine was Josef Hyrtl (1810–1894). An anatomist, Hyrtl was in many ways the antithesis of his Protestant opponent from Berlin. A Catholic from rural Austria, Hyrtl belonged for a time to the reactionary Catholic party and moved in clerical circles ("Hyrtl" 16–17). He had a theatrical flair that came to the fore in his lectures, laced as they were with esoteric Austrian humor (Haeckel 129), as well as occasionally outrageous remarks concerning his fellow professors (Rothschuh 83). Max Neuburger named Hyrtl "the Demosthenes of the autopsy room" (*Entwicklung* 68), and even Ernst Haeckel found the anatomist to be a good though "one-sided" lecturer, a rarity for the University of Vienna medical faculty (136, 129). An anonymous and enthusiastic anatomy student described a not untypical scene: October 1861, the first anatomy lecture of the year: "Suddenly stormy applause, for minutes: the cry 'Hyrtl, Hyrtl, bravo!' Hyrtl had arrived. A sight: the visage of a Roman Emperor serenely glancing at the crowd: finally, a motion of the hand and, as by a stroke of magic, quiet descended" ("Hyrtl" 2). Such descriptions, one imagines, were what led Erna Lesky to conclude that it was "understandable . . . [that] Hyrtl was rejected by followers of Brücke in particular, who were more attracted by that physiologist's sober, matter-of-fact manner" (*School* 215). Surveys of the Viennese Medical School, like those of Lesky and Neuburger, do not and perhaps cannot shed light on controversies such as that between Hyrtl and Brücke. That Hyrtl was unattractive to the physiologist's supporters stemmed not merely from his lecturing style or his unprofessional sense of humor. There were ostensibly irreconcilable philosophical differences between these two "colorful characters," both of whom were "teachers and scientists of outstanding quality" (Vogl 293).

Hyrtl, whose anatomy laboratory "shipped specimens throughout the world" (Johnston 224), and whose textbook went into twenty-two editions (Vogl 293), assumed his professorship at Vienna in 1845, and four years later lent his support to Brücke's candidacy. Similar to Brücke, but to a more limited degree, Hyrtl was a varied and serious scholar: he could summarize his lectures for foreign students in Italian, Hungarian, or Czech, and was conversant with world literature, history, and Hebrew ("Hyrtl" 5). The anatomist had considered surgery as a career, but his reaction to the bleeding involved in operations compelled him to change his plans ("Hyrtl" 4).

Vienna was the better for Hyrtl's decision, for a good part of the Second Viennese School's reputation derived from Hyrtl's having "perfected the techniques of anatomy" (Johnston 224). Up to the middle of the nineteenth century, anatomy and physiology were taught as one subject: through study of comparative anatomy, many morphologists of the time hoped to discover the physiological functions of organs (Rothschuh 85–86). Hyrtl wrote that "anatomy is not supposed to concern itself with the external appearance of the organs only. Its tendency is to unravel the enigma of the functions" (Lesky, *School* 461).

The initial disagreement between Hyrtl and Brücke concerned the location of the kennel for the dogs required by the physiologist's experiments. Hyrtl contended that the barking disturbed him, but more likely he was distressed at the function served by the animals. He wrote to his friend Rudolf Wagner on February 21, 1855: "I am doing badly. The stall containing twenty-four starving dogs, which, despite my request, stands before my window, has brought my own nothingness to consciousness, and I must think of my own departure. People will be excused who cannot tolerate the howling of dogs which are being starved for experimental purposes. And people will be excused who lose their composure when animals with torn-out entrails are dragged to the flaying-cart before their residences" (Rothschuh 83). Hyrtl's response was aggressive and unrelenting. He used every available opportunity to attack Brücke's theory concerning the circulation of blood in the heart, contained in the address, "Physiologische Bemerkungen über die Arteriae Coronariae Cordis" (November 30, 1854), and to condemn the physiologist's work in the most belligerent manner. "Hyrtl's malice," Rothschuh has written, "is hardly to be outdone" (85).

Brücke wrote to Du Bois-Reymond describing what sounds like one of Hyrtl's rude jokes. "He relates that I have ripped off all the lavatory doors so the stink will penetrate everywhere and pester him" (*Briefe* 90). And on March 20, 1855, he informed his friend that he was preparing a written defense because Hyrtl had threatened to spoil his stay in Vienna (Rothschuh 83). Yet the issue here, as Rothschuh has noted, was not the barking of dogs or the heart's circulatory path. Nor was it simply the clash of two strong personalities insisting that each possessed the truth. The case of Hyrtl versus Brücke involved several key issues of the medical and philosophical scene of the mid-nineteenth century and beyond (Rothschuh 85).

Behind a disagreement over the efficacy of vivisection and experimentation with animals in general, was the debate, still current at mid-century, between vitalists and mechanists. The kernel of vitalism, that there was a "life force" (Rothschuh 88) could be viewed as a remnant of *Naturphilosophie*. Rothschuh observed that Hyrtl became famous during a period in which hardly anyone doubted the operation of such a life force, and added that "very often accompanying this vitalism, as with Hyrtl, was a strong reservation concerning animal experimentation and vivisection" (88).

Johnston was somewhat inaccurate, then, in joining Hyrtl with Rokitansky and Skoda as a leader of the New School. Though he may have "scoffed at therapy" (Johnston 226), and though, as Lesky submitted, "his methods . . . were strictly empirical [and]. . . in this respect Hyrtl was a follower of the new exact natural science, and a true member of the Rokitansky school," Hyrtl viewed anatomy simply as "philosophical science." In so doing, Lesky continued, "it is obvious that . . . Hyrtl was heir to the Romantic way of thinking and that his philosophical needs found satisfaction in comparative anatomy" (*School* 213).

Hyrtl's vitalism was almost diametrically opposite to the outlook of Brücke and other members of the so-called Helmholtz School, who were determined to explain natural phenomena as results of the interplay of physical forces. For Rothschuh this school represented the "voice of scientific progress, against the idealistic-metaphysical interpretation of life of the traditionalists. This controversy," he continued, "far surpasses specialized questions of physiology and medicine. Now we are dealing with world-views" (89).

Rothschuh's assessment continued an exaggeration promoted by Hyrtl's inaugural address upon being elected Rektor (October 1, 1864). For his talk Hyrtl chose the title "Die materialistische Welt-anschauung unserer Zeit." He suggested that the extreme materialism of his time was an over-reaction to the sway of *Naturphiloso-phie* at the beginning of the century ("Materialistische Weltan-schauung" 10). So extreme were the consequences of unmitigated materialism that even its advocates were frightened, for nothing less than existing moral sensibilities were threatened ("Weltan-schauung" 10). Hyrtl then moved on to consider the validity of a facet of the extreme materialist position: was the soul merely the product of a brain totally in the service of undeviating organic laws? The anatomist believed that dissection techniques and neuro-anatomical microscopy had almost reached the limits of what they could accomplish, and still science had not detected the machinery of ideation. Even an exact knowledge of the anatomy of individual ganglion cells, however, would not help to explain how brain cells, given their material conditions, had originally been stimulated to operate or in what way they contained the basis for thought ("Weltanschauung" 13-14). Materialism, in Hyrtl's argument, was insufficient to explain a first cause.

After rejecting phrenology (15-17), Hyrtl argued for the notion of freedom of thought. If, as both materialists and idealists maintained, force were a property of matter, then the same matter could possess only the same forces, and the same forces could only call identical effects into existence. Such reasoning was refuted by the very diversity of intellectual life ("Weltanschauung" 19). Moreover, humans create, in the independence of their thought, things without the necessary consistency of natural laws, things which may even express themselves in antitheses. From this observation, Hyrtl concluded that "freedom of thought is something metaphysical, as it expresses itself essentially outside the order of nature and her laws" ("Weltanschauung" 20).

The anatomist continued his attack upon the materialist world-view by noting that pathological observation of the brain in autopsies had added little to the theory that the brain and soul were identical (21). Further, rational life was not the result of physical life. As evidence, Hyrtl cited the case of a Laura Bridgman who lost both vision and hearing at age eighteen months, and taste and smell four months later. Not only was a physician able to raise the child as a rational being, but, by training her intellect (*Geist*) was able to raise her above ordinary people. The consequence of this experience was clear: "Man's intellectual development could not be grounded in the crowd of received sense-impressions" (23).

Hyrtl's argument ultimately came to rest upon a Platonic foundation, in his denial of the contention that the soul died with the body. When a watch broke, more was left than the metal. The Idea remained; it remained "even were all the watches of the world destroyed," for the watch-idea was not the effect of the watch material but rather the principle of the material's use. Similarly, the human being was not the effect of its flesh and blood but the representative of the thought whose spatial expression the body was. "This thought existed before the human-material (*Menschenstoff*) and will remain after him. It is immortal" (26).

This final assertion of a power higher than humanity exemplified Rothschuh's contention that the controversy between Hyrtl and Brücke revolved about the "highest goods of the older generation and . . . the new values of the young" (89). We have seen that Brücke, despite his Protestantism, and despite the special place he reserved for art, viewed man as simply a specific type of organism. Another of Johannes Müller's famous students, Rudolf Virchow, had argued that, for the scientist, transcendence was an "aberration" of the human mind: "the scientific perspective can no longer exist with ecclesiastical belief, philosophical transcendence, and medical insipidity: it has declared the humane in humans to be sovereign, and the earth to be man's heaven" (Rothschuh 89). Just as Virchow's sentiments might be in part reminiscent of those of Karl Marx, so Hyrtl projected that a total triumph of the materialist world-view would have vast political consequences.

First the anatomist lists the materialist's opinion of various cherished beliefs, for examples, "our civilization is only the necessary result of our egoism," and "the idea of a highest being is mindless fear of natural forces." Then Hyrtl warns his listeners of the likely outcome of the spread of such radical notions. They might not be untrue, but most of the populace required consolation, and it was precisely this quality which materialist ideology lacked. The result of widespread dissemination of materialist views could only be revolution (Rothschuh 90).

Hyrtl's elaborate and gloomy forecast might strike one as excessive, as it did an anonymous feuilleton-writer in the *Wiener medizinische Wochenschrift* of October 8, 1864. The writer objected to Hyrtl's use of the most extreme form of materialism, which only existed, if at all, "in the heads of a few zealots" ("Professor Hyrtl's Rektorsrede" 1). Investigation bears out the criticism of the feuilletonist. Franz Husteda observed of Du Bois-Reymond that "he was quite clear about the insuperable limits of the mechanical approach . . . he explicitly admitted that mental phenomena cannot be derived from and understood in terms of the physical and physiological processes in the brain and nervous system" (421).

Frank Sulloway, in his *Freud, Biologist of the Mind,* was careful to differentiate between Brücke and his colleagues, and the truly radical materialismsespoused by men like Karl Vogt and Ludwig Brückner. "Brücke," he noted, "showed a sophisticated, and far from purely 'mechanical' interest in higher mental functioning" (66).

Yet, given the tenor of Virchow's statement above, and Brücke's own confession of faith in materialism from the Introduction of his textbook, one cannot accuse Hyrtl of mere shadow-boxing. In the event, to cite Peter Amacher, "the triumph of materialism [was] . . . general," while the "attitude of the Helmholtz school, with its insistence on descriptions of organic processes in mechanical terms, was preeminent only in Germany" (37).

Despite their own vast philosophical differences, both Brücke and Hyrtl practiced the empirical medicine of the Second Viennese Medical School, while the former seemed to share the skeptics' predilection for an anti-metaphysical approach. The influence of Rokitansky was even more pronounced, in both the philosophical and medical spheres, in the case of psychiatrist Theodor Meynert (1833–1892), who, like Brücke, taught both Freud and Schnitzler.

Meynert, like Brücke, was a man of many parts, and in touch with artists and philosophers of his time, as his daughter vividly portrayed in her biography, *Theodor Meynert und seine Zeit.* The subtitle of the book, which translates to, "On the intellectual history of Austria in the second half of the nineteenth century," was not hyperbolic in its claim of scope, as Lesky has attested (*School* 339). A reading of Meynert's work quickly reveals a widely educated man, "not only in specialized scientific areas, in this case including psychology and philosophy, but also in that realm quite distant from brain mechanics, art and poetry" (Dorer 143).

The relationship between Meynert and Rokitansky was personal as well as professional: even Meynert's wife loved the pathologist (Stockert-Meynert 34). According to Fritz Hartmann, the psychiatrist was himself especially drawn both by Rokitansky's spiritual elevation and his specialized knowledge (2). Nobel laureate

Julius Wagner-Jauregg noted Rokitansky's sympathy and support for his young colleague. Meynert quickly found in Rokitansky "the patron of so many talents, a guardian who opened for him a promising career" ("Skoda und Meynert" 6). For his part, Meynert advanced the cause of specialization urged by Rokitansky. The pathologist's "search for anatomical localization bore its last fruits in the neuroanatomy of" Meynert (Lesky, *School* 334).

Indeed, Meynert's professional starting point was an insistence that "psychiatry be given the character of a scientific discipline by determining its anatomical basis" (Lesky, *School* 335). For this true disciple of Rokitansky, mental disease, like bodily disorders, had a material, that is, physical explanation, for which one had to search. Meynert's psychiatric textbook carried the subtitle, "Clinic of diseases of the forebrain, based upon its construction, functions, and maintenance." G. Anton observed that Meynert's map of the brain's anatomy, gained by diligent effort, was consulted as a battle plan in the estimation of both gross diseases of the brain as well as psychoses (5). Further, Meynert attempted to explain the unclear mechanisms of psychoses physiologically, on the basis of the interplay of higher and lower neuronal stations (*Nervenstationen*) (Anton 6).

Meynert's initial presupposition and the manner in which he sought to reach his goal were what raised him, in Wagner-Jauregg's opinion, above all other neuroanatomists, that is, Meynert's "conviction, that one could only understand an organ's construction after considering its function ("Skoda und Meynert" 7–8). Rokitansky surely would have been in complete agreement with the sentiment Meynert expressed early in his textbook. "'Treatment of the Soul'" was to be disdained because it "entailed 'more than we can accomplish and transcends the bounds of accurate scientific investigation'" (Johnston 231).

Both in a lecture of 1880, "Über die Gefühle," and in "Über die Gesetzmäßigkeit des menschlichen Denkens" of a year later, Meynert attacked the notion of free will in language reminiscent of Rokitansky: "All philosophy, all human acceptance of wisdom so far as history spans, has really brought to light only two conclusions in which the outlook of those who have made use of the thought of all mankind differs from that of the common man. One is that everything in the world is only appearance and the appearance is not identical with the essence of things; the second is that even the freedom we feel in ourselves is only apparent" (Jones 1, 400–401). Meynert's rationale, Jones continued, was simply that we had not yet developed the tools to follow the "finest details" of the brain's processes. Meynert concluded, according to Jones, that "the apparent freedom is really based on law, therefore on necessity" (1, 401). Sigmund Freud, as we will see, agreed with Meynert's assessment of free will, while the implication that free will, however illusory, was necessary for social order, was shared by Arthur Schnitzler.

As was the case with Rokitansky, Meynert's dedication to scientific objectivity and to explanations based on physical evidence, carried with it an aloofness towards, if not a disdain for, his patients (Johnston 231). Beyond sharing Rokitansky's point of view regarding the business of medicine, Meynert seems to have adopted and then evolved his mentor's world-view. This tendency was exemplified in the psychiatrist's collection of varyingly accessible essays, *Sammlung von populär-wissenschaftlichen Vorträgen über den Bau und die Leistungen des Gehirns,* published in the year of his death, and a posthumously published book of poetry, *Gedichte* (1905). Thus, like Rokitansky, Meynert also expressed his views outside the scientific arena.

The earliest of Meynert's essays in the *Sammlung,* delivered on March 24, 1868, bore the title "The Significance of the Brain for Conceptual Life" (*Vorstellungsleben*). The lecture addressed the issue of brain/mind (or "soul": *Seele*) relationship which Hyrtl had approached in his inaugural speech as Rektor some four years earlier. Meynert, taking the materialist tack, argued the opposite side of the case. He located the brain and mind together, coexisting within the two hemispheres of the brain-matter (*Sammlung* 4). Human intelligence, Meynert said, was conditioned by the ratio of the weight of the two hemispheres vis-à-vis total brain weight (7). Anatomic comparison taught that the mind made demands upon parts of the brain corresponding to the wealth of its conceptual contents. Thus, the section of the brain's hemispheres relating to a particular type of concept will be larger in animals or humans demonstrating a proclivity for that type of conceptualization (9).

The seeming equation of mind and intelligence drawn by Meynert was then given direct expression: "The hemispheres of the gross brain are not just a condition of mental (or 'spiritual': *Seelenvorgänge*) processes, they are the site of the mind itself." Meynert supported this essentially materialist view with clinical evidence. "First . . . the destruction of no other brain part save the hemispheres destroys mental (or 'spiritual') capabilities, and second, the form of the hemispheres meets the demands of psychical transpirations" (*Sammlung* 10).

Meynert continued his discussion by positing the evolutionary nature of neuroanatomy. The circumference of the human skull was still growing, due to its activity. From this observation the psychiatrist concluded that humanity's high place in the animal kingdom, based upon its intellectual achievement, was owing solely to our own efforts: "Disregarding all opinions concerning descent, one thing remains firm: no otherworldly power directly raised humanity to its height of psychical functioning . . . the highest value of his organism [i.e., his great mind] was bestowed by humanity upon itself" (*Sammlung* 15).

As though to mitigate a conclusion which in its atheism might have struck his audience as negative, Meynert ended his remarks by offering two routes to avoid the pessimism of Schopenhauer's world-view. The first, the practice of Indian asceticism, he rejected as unfruitful. It would lead to "world-historical atrophy" and a weakening of brain development. Meynert's suggestion was youthfully optimistic: one was to raise oneself to useful work and set intellectual effort as one's goal for happiness (*Sammlung* 16).

No such simple solution was offered or even sought after in later essays. Meynert's memorial address for Rokitansky (1878) showed the proximity of their perspectives. Meynert first summarized Rokitansky's contributions to psychiatry, both indirect – the objective point of view offered in his pathology text – and direct – his contribution of corpses to the psychiatric clinic. The psychiatrist then portrayed Rokitansky's world-view, offering without objection the approach to life and science discussed earlier in this chapter (*Sammlung* 76).

Meynert submitted that realism (read "skepticism") simply served as the abbreviated expression of the methods of Rokitansky's objective science but did not represent a *Weltanschauung* (*Sammlung* 76). In the positive manner of Meynert's encapsulation, the genre of his presentation notwithstanding, one can read his own movement away from an earlier extreme materialism: "Rokitansky, as no one before him, independently developed idealistic philosophy out of science and out of his objectively rooted thought process. The teachings, 'what should one think of things,' and 'that things also possess an inner, non-observable and an experientially transcendent being' were actually developed by Rokitansky in his concise, significant presentation completely from the core of his own individual observation" (*Sammlung* 77). Rokitansky's essay on the solidarity of all animal life also won Meynert's approbation. The psychiatrist cited long passages from the work and added that "other parts compare the position of animals and humans to other humans with a razor-sharp truth" (*Sammlung* 79).

The conclusion which Rokitansky drew in his essay concerning animal life was that compassion (*Mitleid*) was the key to overcoming suffering. That same ability to "suffer with," which Meynert included in his category of accessory conception (*Nebenvorstellung*), merited high praise as "one of the noblest phenomena of human accessory conceptions" (*Sammlung* 75). Nevertheless the psychiatrist saw an inherent danger in compassion. Without discussion he offered the insight, in the address of 1885, "Über den Wahn," that in the notion of compassion "is found the thought of guilt for the other's suffering" (*Sammlung* 96).

Meynert must have been confronted with a frustrating dilemma: what both Rokitansky and he saw as a meritorious quality evolved from the feeling of guilt. Perhaps the attempt to find a way to escape this difficulty led the psychiatrist, in the address of 1888, "Gehirn und Gesittung," to go several steps further, up to and then beyond Rokitansky's position in his public utterances.

Like Rokitansky, Meynert accepted a Darwinian interpretation of the natural world, and his definition of *Gesittung* was a human's posture vis-à-vis other creatures. "These social relations," he wrote, "in the deepest sense, find their start, their motivation . . . in the struggles for existence that, in Darwin's theory (*Lehre*), unavoidably follows from the propensity of all organisms to propagate at an intense rate" (*Sammlung* 191). The extent to which humanity moderated this struggle for existence represented the level of its morality (or "culture": *Gesittung*). Thus, morality for Meynert, involved the conscious agitating against what he conceded to be the natural impulse for self-preservation and continuation. In its elevated conception, but also in its proven feasibility, Christianity, for Meynert, stood alone in offering the best possible morality within this struggle (*Sammlung* 142).

Advocacy of Christian morality as a means of mitigating the ruthless Darwinian scenario went beyond Rokitansky's argument: the pathologist stopped short in positing compassion as the best, but still unsatisfactory, means of overcoming suffering. Meynert's analysis continued by accepting Rokitansky's stipulation of hunger and motility as the two great motivations in organisms. as well as the drive for their satisfaction through aggressive activity (*Sammlung* 144).

Far worse, for the good of humanity, was the prevalence of parasitism. Meynert was once again on new ground in discussing this phenomenon which, both in the animal kingdom and in human morality, "is the alien . . . the evil. Its principal expression is slavery of all degrees, the exploitation of the work of another" (*Sammlung* 167). Meynert was not interested in explaining the political dimensions of the point here raised, rather, he advocated "mutualism," the very antithesis of parasitism, as the "distant goal of human morality." Moral (cultural) progress was, by definition, the repression (*Verdrängung*) of parasitism by mutualism or reciprocity. Further, reciprocity was itself a synonym for brotherliness, so Meynert concluded, the level of all progressive morality truly lay in the fundamental thought of Christianity (*Sammlung* 167). Perhaps the psychiatrist was further attracted to Christianity as the means by which the guilt wrought by compassion might be assuaged, but he did not say so explicitly.

The remainder of Meynert's lecture "Gehirn und Gesittung" was also of some significance, for here he was at pains to develop another concept introduced in his earlier essay, "Über die Gefühle," namely, his division of the human psyche into two selves (or "egos": *ich*). In the earlier address Meynert concerned himself with discussing the primary self, that part of the human mind that dealt with sense impressions and memory. The primary self was associated with the child: it represented the first step in human development (Dorer 140). The simpler a person's range of contemplation, and the poorer his intellectual capacity (*geistiger Inhalt*), the more predominant was the primary self in ideation. The consciousness of this type of primary self was almost solely concerned with bodily sensations. According to Meynert, "maximum defense of both thought and deed is aimed against death, and against the destruction of the primary self" (*Sammlung* 65).

In the course of time, however, came the incorporation of other images, closely associated with the person but independent of bodily sensations. Here again, compassion served as an example: "The suffering of other people excites his emotions to compassion. His defense sets itself against the bad feelings of the other, the aggression of his activity seeks to reinstate the other's happiness" (*Sammlung* 66). Such representations (*Bilder*) became just as closely connected to the cortex as one's own reminiscences of the womb. Meynert concluded from this that the self combining with the external world constituted an inseparable, and a further, individuality, an expanded or secondary self. This individuality was extended by the possession of intimately bound persons and aesthetic and scientific thoughts and deeds. The formerly imperative defense of one's body was now mitigated. Beliefs like fatherland, duty, or honor become part of the expanded self, so that one's opinion that the body's defense was necessary for the retention of individuality collapsed. The greater a person's commitment to such other-directed convictions, the more powerful became the appearance of his freedom (*Sammlung* 66): but, as was mentioned earlier, this freedom was illusory.

The role of the secondary self was further discussed in Meynert's essay concerning morality, in the context of parasitism. This more advanced self had a tendency to want to become part of a greater whole, and concepts such as the common good or the welfare of the State might well be included in the development of association processes. Though the socialization of the self was parasitical to the extent that it relied upon others, for Meynert the secondary self was rather associated with the desirable aims of mutualism. It, like the primary self, was constantly growing. It appropriated aggressive emotions, which, according to Meynert, could also be termed happy emotions, and it defended its realm (*Sammlung* 171).

Meynert argued that during this complicated development, personal morality evolved into conscience, "which is a collective name for very different processes. Conscience is at its lowest level fear, at its second level compassion" (*Sammlung* 177). Indeed, the psychiatrist opined that a state organized upon this very elevated plane of mutualism would be above anything yet attained by human society. There existed for Meynert, ultimately, the possibility of a third stage of conscience consisting of a self-love, but now in connection with an advanced secondary self. The self-image of such a secondary self entailed a certain ease which could be identical with that wrought by the beautiful, the good, and the true. This very advanced self then became part of the unity represented by the pleasure in self, truth, etc., and worked toward its satisfaction. Meynert noted that this unity's gratification was quite distant from the impulses of the primary self (*Sammlung* 177).

An essay of 1885, "Über den Wahn," addressed the problem of the psyche that did not follow the normal path of development. Significantly, it was in this work that Meynert turned briefly to a discussion of folk religion in the context of societal madness. The ancient's conceptualization of the deities began with the notion that, just as humans consciously acted upon nature, so must there be a consciousness behind the natural phenomena affecting man. This anthropomorphization of the gods continued with the attribution to them of human accessory conceptions (*Nebenvorstellungen*) such as compassion, and their categorization along the lines of humanly conceived hierarchies (*Sammlung* 95). Human illness, Meynert maintained, did not create any more insane visions than were evoked by the original relationship between man and nature, marked as they were by man's megalo- and persecution mania (*Sammlung* 97).

A society's common delusion was modeled by its myths. Beyond a shared mythology, Meynert continued, mimicry was a necessary influence in the construction of a strong state. Only a small number of people rose above mere thought imitation, so the effect of mimicry was widespread and powerful. Indeed, Meynert believed mimicry was the source of madness in folklife, which played a large role in contagious illnesses, as, for example, the dance-frenzy (*Tanzwut*) of the *Totentanz* following plagues of the Middle Ages (*Sammlung* 97).

Many of the ideas found in Meynert's *Sammlung* were made more accessible by the psychiatrist in his poetry. He wrote: "One thing would have to interest a poet in this: namely, how a person, constrained in his behavior and neglected, still develops his inner force, how this, with an incalculable store of adaptability, realizes its goal, and, in this realization and recognition unintentionally serves the best ends. And how it is not always in the mirror of societal norms that one finds the right way but, rather, on the contrary . . ." (Stockert-Meynert 243). Yet, in his own poetry, Meynert did not stray far afield, nor can one perceive the rather optimistic attitude of the citation. Many of his creations were quite directly didactic, rather singlemindedly forcing the reader to reach Meynert's conclusion. Nor could Meynert's poems be held in the same awe as those of a professional craftsman. He, like Brücke in his paintings, was expressing himself in a medium he found comfortable. His daughter said that rather than great art, his poetic work reflected the thinker and philosopher (Anton 1).

Much of Meynert's poetry was in fact suffused with the pessimism and determinism of his world-view. The poem "Transformed" (*Verwandelt*), by juxtaposing friends with the dreams of one's youth, depicts a deep disillusionment. The narrator had thought his friendships solid, like columns, while his dreams were changing and unstable as clouds. But now instead, "those friends of mine, a youthful dream, dispersed / The youthful dream alone remains my friend" (*Gedichte* 62). The psychiatrist's philosophical idealism is reflected in "On the Cat," which reveals the "true" and rather sinister nature of the household pet: "Cruel, but timidly coaxing, aware only of dark power / You drink the milk of frailty, but blood is your desire" (19–20).

"The Hunter" describes a hunter who leaves peaceful fields to stalk game in the wilderness: the game escapes and he is left to die alone on the cliffs. Meynert continued by clarifying the moral to be learned: "We hunt for life's fleeting game / Restless, to the furthest extent / We don't know to whom the hunting applies / We ourselves are the booty" (82). Nor could one actually have a great deal of hope for human improvement or progress. In "Soldiers' Lot" the psychiatrist-poet briefly described four comrades, three of whom are unhappy as soldiers, while the fourth is quite content. He relates: "I'm chained by no love, bound by no place . . . ." Not unexpectedly, considering Meynert's outlook, it is the fourth, the cold unfeeling man who survives: "The fourth, he saw them lying there, the three, / Shrugged his shoulders and marched on by –" (3–4). Perhaps the ultimate expression of Meynert's pessimism was reserved for the poem "Vanquished" (*Bezwungen*), in which he boldly addressed the issue of what was to be done if Fate were simply against one. "If Fate truly holds your arm bound/ When a common hurdle becomes a bear-pit –/ For such woe I've found no consolation / For you there remains no motto save: 'Die or kill!' " (78).

Even the transcendental possibilities of imagination are presented in a negative light in Meynert's poem "Moss." The imagery is of a gloomy landscape from which moss offers the only relief. Analogously, the imagination covers over life's fallowness with a colorful carpet. In nature, the elk (*Elentier*) looks for its meal in the snow, on ground sweetly mossy, while man seeks consolation for the misery of life (*Elendtrost*) in imagination (37). The rigid parallelism of the not particularly attractive moss with imagination, and the elk (= deer = faint-hearted) with man, and the choice of winter for the transpiration of the poem, reveal Meynert's negative point of view. In the psychiatrist's poetry, as was the case in Rokitansky's thought, it was compassion which was seen to offer some relief from life's sorrows. In the poem "Stages of the Spirit" (*Gemüt*), compassion was granted the highest place: "Rich is the beggar, freezing along the way / Who feels empathy at the sobbing of a girl" (91--92). Interesting from the perspective of Meynert's commitment to compassion, at least in his writings, was the poem "Reassurance" (*Beruhigung* 124-125), a panegyric of stoic ideals in both the avoidance of extremes and suppression of emotions.

This tension between compassion and the desire to maintain control over one's emotions, or more precisely the need to retain a detached objectivity, was, judging from the evidence, both a deepseated and significant part of Meynert's personality, and had broader applications. The emphasis upon compassion found in the writings of Meynert and Rokitansky might be seen as contrasting with their usual depictions as reserved and cool in their professional relations. The contrast was particularly striking in the case of Meynert. For Rokitansky, despite his often emotionless face, nevertheless possessed the "stamp of great kind-heartedness" (Kussmaul 285). Nor was Meynert's opinion that Rokitansky had "true love of humanity" (*Sammlung* 81) disputed.

While recognizing its importance, Meynert, it should be recalled, did not endow compassion with the ultimate significance assigned it by the pathologist. Still, when one reads Lesky's assessment: "Meynert was propelled by the elan of the natural-scientific movement and . . . regarded psychiatry and its 'patient material,' the mentally diseased, mainly as material for exact scientific research" (*School* 340), "compassionate" seems a totally inappropriate adjective to apply to the psychiatrist's attitude. Yet, inexplicably, as Arthur Schnitzler reported in his autobiography *Jugend in Wien*, Meynert would often stubbornly attempt to use rational argumentation to coax incurable patients to abandon fixed ideas

(260). This does not sound like the action of a totally detached scientist.

In the end Meynert's insistence on the importance of compassion vis-à-vis his detached attitude to patients can be viewed as a variation on the theme of the role of the physician. Does the researcher accomplish more for humanity than the clinician? Meynert's achievement can be contrasted with the more outwardly humane Feuchtersleben. "Meynert made Feuchtersleben's art of healing of the psyche into a science of the 'structure and functions of the brain and the spinal cord with regard to their diseases,' i.e., psychiatry became part of applied anatomy and physiology" (Lesky, *School* 344). As in the case of Rokitansky, Meynert's dedication to science, objective science, coexisted with his consideration of the philosophies of Kant and Schopenhauer "whose acquaintance he made partly through his teacher and friend Carl Rokitansky" (Dorer 129).

Johnston maintained that Meynert typified therapeutic nihilism (232), but it would be more accurate to say that he embodied therapeutic skepticism. In Meynert the major questions facing the Second Viennese Medical School came together. His "passion for taxonomy," according to Johnston, "exemplified the obstacles awaiting anyone who would apply Brücke's method to psychiatry" (232). Thus, not only do we see in Meynert that tension between theory and praxis, but we also confront in him a participant in the debate concerning the validity of materialism/determinism.

CHAPTER TWO

Sigmund Freud, Determinist and Skeptic

Sigmund Freud's relationship to, and opinions of, medicine were as complex as his interaction with and emotions for the medical faculty of the University of Vienna. Statements concerning the art of healing in Freud's *Autobiographical Study* all reflect a lack of dedication. Almost at the very start the author admitted that "neither at that time, nor indeed in my later life, did I feel any particular predilection for the career of a physician" (13), and a bit later, "the various branches of medicine proper, apart from psychiatry, had no attraction for me. I was decidedly negligent in pursuing my medical studies" (16). Henri Ellenberger has noted that it took Freud the unusually long period of eight years (1873–1881) to complete his training (430). In fact, in the 1935 "Postscript" to his sketch Freud spoke of his career as "a lifelong detour through the natural sciences, medicine and psychotherapy." From what had he veered? : from, "the cultural problems which had fascinated me long before" (137). Siegfried Bernfeld wrote that "it was not medicine he was after . . . becoming a doctor was no ideal, it rather meant a defense against his ambition to play a leading part in politics . . . ("Freud's Earliest Theories" 355). Freud, Bernfeld observed in another article, felt the need to be great, an opinion shared by Marthe Robert (*Sigmund Freud: Zwischen Moses und Oedipus* (64). At age seventeen Freud wrote a friend that he feared mediocrity (Bernfeld, "Freud's Scientific Beginnings" 3).

Whether as a means for attaining greatness or merely because the scientific method proffered "the best means of gratifying" his true proclivity for examining cultural problems (*Study* 14), Freud became a doctor/scientist and publicly maintained a dedication to science until his death, as evidenced by his paean to the scientific *Weltanschauung* in the *New Introductory Lectures* of 1932 (158–182). Philip Rieff has noted that "Freud was easily converted to the Darwinian gospel and a lifelong faith in science (*Freud: The Mind of the Moralist* 282). The important distinction between medicine and science, as was developed in Chapter One (praxis versus theory, respectively), will be addressed below.

It was in Brücke's physiology laboratory that the student "found rest and satisfaction – and men, too, whom I could respect and take as my models" (*Study* 16). There is a debate concerning the impact on Freud of the materialistic world-view which was thought to have dominated Brücke's laboratory; that issue will be addressed below. Beyond the plausibility of such a fundamental influence, Brücke, after whom Freud's son, Ernst, was named (Robert, *Die Revolution der Psychoanalyse* 89), likely affected Freud in three less significant ways as well. George Rosen, in "Freud and Medicine in Vienna," saw the young Freud as casting about for a set of values. He found this in Brücke's laboratory and simultaneously learned restraint in philosophical speculation from his master (24). Jones related Freud's distrust or "perhaps . . . even . . . fear" of philosophical speculation, against which Freud found "scientific discipline to be the most effective check" (1, 324). Rokitansky had a similar "problem." Miciotto wrote that the pathologist "was possibly caught between his desire as a pathological anatomist to strictly adhere to his materialistic inclinations, and a very fundamental predisposition toward romantic speculations. The result . . . was the creation of the occasional dilemma which made painfully obvious the incomplete resolution of these ideologies" (185). In his *Autobiographical Study* Freud admitted that "in the work of my later years . . . I have given free rein to the inclination which I kept down for so long to speculation. . . ." (109). This is by no means the only similarity Freud shared with the cofounder of the Second Viennese Medical School. They both hailed from what is now Czechoslovakia, and more significantly, as we will see, shared an attachment to the philosophy of Arthur Schopenhauer. Freud also straddled two worlds as far as his reading preferences were concerned. According to Jack Spector, he "tended to prefer the empirical and pragmatic Eighteenth Century English writers . . . but was also attached to the Romantics' theme of dream/reality dualism" (8).

Brücke also served as the model of tenacity for his student, according to Jones, especially in the early struggles over the sexual etiology of neuroses. The physiologist had shown "the same tenacious adherence to new ideas as Freud was to do" (1, 274). Yet, in the realm of art, Brücke's example, which Freud followed again, was in the opposite direction. We have seen Brücke's love of the old masters of visual art, especially of Leonardo and Michelangelo. Spector observed that Freud's taste in art was at first identical to Brücke's, with the exception of Freud's affinity for Egyptian and archaic Greek art (12–13). Freud, too, was overwhelmed by Michelangelo, especially by his "Moses." Of it, he wrote: "No piece of statuary has ever made a stronger impression on me . . ." (McGrath 311). And both men shared a dislike for the "modern" art of their respective periods (Spector 12–13).

Freud also possessed that broad education of nineteenth century European professionals, which, as in the case of Brücke and Meynert, led to wide interests and a great store of diversified knowledge (Amacher 23; Esslin 46). Spector remarked that "like his teachers, with humanist educations, [Freud] sought a pathway leading from his science to art and culture" (9). Freud's late parapsychological works and his admission in the *Autobiographical*

Study offer evidence for Spector's conclusion.

After six years in Brücke's laboratory Freud spent five months of 1882 in the psychiatric clinic of the "great" Meynert, "in whose footsteps I followed with such veneration" (Amacher 21). Meynert, as a psychiatrist and one of Europe's leading neuroanatomists, had a very direct bearing on Freud's professional career. Both Amacher (21–41) and McGrath have examined at some length the influence of Meynert's neuroanatomy upon the founder of psychoanalysis, and the latter has gone on to posit, with good cause, that Freud's was "a substantial intellectual debt [to Meynert] extending well beyond the specifics of brain anatomy" (141).

Freud's relations with Meynert were highly charged emotionally and ended unhappily. In his *Autobiographical Study* Freud first expressed admiration for Meynert, "by whose work and personality I had been greatly struck while ... still a student" (17), and on the very next page, suspicion: "it is possible, too, that I had guessed already that this great man was by no means kindly disposed towards me" (18). The root of animosity probably never will be known with certainty. Jones, not unexpectedly, put the blame squarely on the older man's shoulders (1, 178), hinting at Meynert's envy of Freud's genius (1, 227), and submitting, finally, in a footnote, that: "Meynert, one of the chief opponents, later confessed to Freud on his deathbed that he had himself been a classical case of male hysteria, but had always managed to conceal the fact; incidentally it is known that he was a very erratic and neurotic person and a heavy drinker" (1, 253).

Freud revealed an intense dislike for Meynert in letters to Wilhelm Fliess. On August 29, 1888 he wrote of Meynert, "who in his customary impudent-malicious manner spoke out authoritatively on a topic of which he knows nothing" (Masson 24). Mentioning his *Zur Auffassung der Aphasien* in a letter of May 2, 1891, Freud described his own "very impudent" attitude in daring to "scratch the high and mighty idol Meynert" (Masson 28). And when, following Meynert's death, Freud was graciously allowed to choose a memento from his teacher's library, he wrote to Fliess

(7/12/92) that "the opportunity to select from Meynert's library what future book suited me [was] somehow like a savage drinking mead from his enemy's skull" (Masson 32). Strong language of the type used in Freud's letters to his confidant in Berlin lends credence to the argument that his dispute with Meynert was based on profounder grounds than scientific disagreement. Gustav Lebzeltern argued against Jones' assessment in "Sigmund Freud und Theodor Meynert," by looking for the "deeper reasons" for the two psychiatrists' falling-out. The basis of his thesis, that Freud was more at fault than his teacher, was a dream from Freud's *Interpretation of Dreams,* which McGrath has called the "council dream." Freud perceived in his teacher a father-figure, "against whom his rebellious feelings were directed" (McGrath 305–306). And Lebzeltern posited that "Freud had repressed the hate against his father, and this must necessarily be directed against the father substitute (14). Meynert, for his part, disliked the notion of Freud entering private practice, where, he believed, physicians too often became overly concerned with business matters (Barea 310).

Although the actual "deeper reasons" for the termination of this relationship might contribute to the question at hand, namely, Meynert's influence upon Freud, one must be content to accept Ronald Clark's simple but indisputable conclusion that it was hypnosis which came between the two psychiatrists. When Freud returned from Paris in 1886 he was enthused by the work in hypnosis being done by Jean Martin Charcot. Meynert, as a cursory perusal of his essay, "Über künstliche Störungen des psychischen Gleichgewichts," reveals, had no use for hypnosis, and, as Jones concluded, "he evidently felt that Charcot had seduced Freud from the strict and narrow path of pure science" (1, 257).

As the concluding pages of the last chapter sought to portray, Meynert's outlook, whether expressed in his lectures, essays, or poetry, had been thoroughly impregnated with Schopenhauerian pessimism and philosophical idealism, as had been the case with his mentor, Rokitansky, before him. It was in conveying Schopenhauer's thought to Freud that Meynert, as has only recently been appreciated, played a significant role in shaping Freud's perspective. Ernest Jones did not concern himself with Schopenhauer's possible influence on Freud. He remarked, in discussing Freud's impulse (*Trieb*) theory, that the psychoanalyst seemed to have landed in the position of Schopenhauer, who taught that "death is the goal of life," but had "dexterously extricated himself" (3, 300). Freud himself acknowledged the significance of Schopenhauer's notion of "unconscious 'Will,'" which he equated with the impulses in the mind (Rieff, *Freud: The Mind of the Moralist* 38). Ludwig Marcuse, writing at the same time as Jones, pointed to several parallels between the German philosopher and Austrian psychoanalyst, and described the former as "Freud's greatest ancestor" (35, 54).

In a fuller treatment R. K. Gupta, in his essay of 1980, "Freud and Schopenhauer," has noted four areas of partial or total agreement between the two thinkers. Gupta perceived the similarity of Schopenhauer's "will" and Freud's "id," but stressed the universality of the former concept as opposed to the individual character of the latter. The overriding importance of sex in human motivation was recognized by both, and both presented a "black view of human sexuality and regard[ed] it as an ignoble slavery to nature" (229). Freud's notion of repression, which was first called "defense," based upon Meynert's use of that term, closely resembled a thought expressed by Schopenhauer in his *The World as Will and Representation* (McGrath 148). And Gupta submitted that both Freud and Schopenhauer recognized the dangers to the personality of excessive repression (231).

There appeared to be a direct connection between the approaches to religion of Schopenhauer and Freud. Both Rieff (*Mind* 323) and Gupta depicted the striking similarities of the philosopher's "Dialogue on Religion," and Freud's *Future of an Illusion*. This led Gupta to conclude that it seemed "extremely likely that Freud had read Schopenhauer's work." The fundamental assumption of each discussion was the same: religious belief was "absurd" for rational man (Gupta 232). Yet for the philosopher religion was required "for the sake of culture," while Freud argued that "religion can and must be overcome" (Rieff, *Mind* 324). Further, Meynert's theory of the psyche consisting of two selves (*Ichs*), the primary and secondary, examined in Chapter One, was also based upon Schopenhauer's conception of the individual will. In turn, Meynert's division was found by McGrath to be the root of Freud's distinction between id and ego (145).

Based upon the similarities if not identities that he recorded, Gupta contended that "perhaps it may not be too fanciful to suggest . . . that behind the similarity of views between Schopenhauer and Freud on several subjects . . . there lies a similarity of general attitude towards life," and added, "this attitude may be described as one of disillusionment and despair" (232–233). Yet the point of convergence that best illustrated Gupta's contention was examined only recently by William J. McGrath. In *Freud's Discovery of Psychoanalysis* (1986) McGrath convincingly argued for a profound Schopenhauerian foundation to Freud's thought, based upon Meynert's influence (141–149).

It was related at the end of the last chapter that in Meynert the two great intellectual controversies at the University of Vienna Medical School coalesced. Like Rokitansky, he was firmly rooted in philosophic idealism, and doubt about medicine's efficacy seemed fully consistent with a teaching of the unreliability of our senses to perceive the truth, and the division of the world into appearances and realities. More surprising and at first thought paradoxical was the coexistence of philosophical idealism and determinism. Yet McGrath wrote: "within the Kantian framework there was no contradiction in the belief that the unchangeable, scientifically predictable, material world of nature was also a world of appearances or phenomena" (143), and continued by citing a turn-of-the-century scholar, Wilhelm Jerusalem: "Rokitansky and Meynert as well as Helmholtz and Du Bois-Reymond are firm idealists and true adherents of Kant and Schopenhauer. They are all firmly convinced of the fact that the world which we have before us is only an appearance and that we can never fathom the somewhat hidden essence behind the appearance." In the footnote to this citation, McGrath submitted that the idealist tradition underlay Freud's "two-sided approach to mental activity" (144). This argument was clarified a bit later when McGrath quoted Freud's *On Aphasia* (1891): "The psychic is, therefore, a process parallel to the physiological, 'a dependent concomitant.' Here again, the two worlds were actually one world experienced two ways, the view advanced by Schopenhauer, Meynert . . . and many other leading scientific thinkers" (163).

Interesting differences among Schopenhauer, Meynert, and Freud appear quite rapidly. The philosopher had held that Kant's thing-in-itself was the will, "blind, and irrational" (McGrath 144). According to Jones, Meynert, "like most scientists of the time, considered force to be the noumenal in things" (1, 402). He had argued, as we have seen, against the existence of free will (Jones 1, 401). Klaus Schröter saw Freud's approach to the question of free will as an example of his replacement of a system, that of the Helmholtz school, with a method (153). Freud's approach, as described by Jones, was to investigate the motivation for the human conviction of "freedom of choice" (1, 401). In doing so Freud continued to "carefully avoid any contact with philosophy" (*Autobiographical Study* 114).

Freud, "dialectician that he was," saw the debate concerning freedom of will as asking the wrong question (Schröter 153). The psychoanalyst observed that our sense of freedom was far stronger in trivial decisions than with important ones. In deciding weighty matters we felt our "inner natures" compelling us in a given direction. Yet what actually took place, say, in the choice of a number, was that the decision was left to and made by the unconscious mind. From this Jones concluded, "if unconscious motivation is taken into account, therefore, the rule of determination is of general validity" (1, 401).

That there was a necessary causal chain for everything that occurred was a belief from which, as Jones observed, Freud never departed (1, 50). Such a belief stood behind the enterprise of dream analysis, or the *Psychopathology of Everyday Life,* in which all elements of dreams and every slip of the tongue or hand were held to be significant (Robert, *Revolution* 115). As Schröter emphasized, Freud's determinism actually began where the Helmholtz school's left off (152) and was just opposite to Schnitzler's development, as we will see. Du Bois-Reymond had after all admitted that intellectual processes transcended the laws of causality. The question arises, given Freud's determinism and the climate of therapeutic skepticism in which he received his medical training, as to whether or to what extent Freud viewed psychoanalysis as a therapeutic device.

We have already observed Freud's reluctance to become a medical doctor, and he has been cited as showing a lack of concern for his patients. Abraham Kardiner attributed the following remark to Freud: "I am not basically interested in therapy. I usually find I am engaged in any particular case – with the theoretical problems with which I happen to be interested at the time" (Clark 81). Yet, as Freud observed in the 1935 "Postscript" to his *Autobiographical Study,* he "never ceased . . . analytic work," and treated patients until almost the end of his life. And in his relatively late essay, "The Question of Lay-Analysis" (1926), Freud expended much effort in an explanation of the therapeutic goals of his science.

In the "Question" Freud described his therapeutic aim as consisting of the restoration of the ego, its liberation from restrictions, and its being given command over the id. "Our whole technique," he wrote, "is directed to this aim" (115–116). In this essay Freud also addressed a theme that appealed to Schnitzler in both his *Aphorismen* and a short story, "Flucht in die Finsternis": illness as irresponsibility. Sickness could be used, Freud noted, to account for incompetence or failure; it could be employed in "extorting proof of love from family members" (136). Despite the fact that such motivations were fairly obvious, the patient's ego often "knows nothing of the whole concatenation of the motives and actions involved" (137). Significantly, in terms of the discussion of therapeutic skepticism, the question was raised whether it might not be better to refrain from treating "these difficult people" altogether. Freud's response says a great deal about his own outlook. He disapproved of the suggestion and continued: "It is undoubtedly a more proper line to accept the complications of life rather than struggle against them. It may be true that not every neurotic whom we treat is worth the expenditure of an analysis, but there are some very valuable individuals among them as well. We must set ourselves the goal of bringing it about that as few human beings as possible enter civilized life with such a defective mental equipment" (136). These are hardly the sentiments of a would-be savior, nor do they reflect the beliefs of a totally disinterested party. This passage does not contradict Freud's remark to Kardiner, but it does lend a quite different light to Freud's work. Rieff put the matter succinctly in writing that Freud "was interested in problems not patients, in the mechanics of civilization not in programs of mental health" (*Mind* xxiii), a view echoed by Bettelheim: "whatever practical benefits may be derived from psychoanalysis, they were only incidental to its cultural achievements, which were paramount to Freud. . . ." (63–64).

The real core of Freud's 1926 essay was his contention that nonphysicians be allowed to practice psychoanalysis. In this argument one can observe how far Freud had come to deviate from his training at the University of Vienna Medical School. In his medical education, Freud wrote, the physician acquired "more or less the opposite of what he would need for psychoanalysis. His attention has been directed to objectively ascertainable facts of anatomy . . . the problem of life is brought into his field of vision so far as it has hitherto been explained to us by the play of forces which can also be observed in inanimate nature . . . medicine is not concerned with the study of the higher intellectual functions . . ." (146–147). One wonders if Freud was aware of the paradox involved in these sentiments: the founder of psychoanalysis arguing that what had been his own medical background was inadequate for a psychoanalyst! Despite this rejection of materialist science as a proper background for psychoanalysts, Freud continued by postulating the "intricate connection" between the physical and mental, and by expressing anticipation of the day, still quite distant, when paths leading from organic biology and chemistry to neurotic phenomena would be opened (148; Worbs 89). A number of elements in psychoanalytic theory and practice might be traced to the tradition of therapeutic skepticism. For example, the use of the ill, in this case the neurotic, to give clues concerning the healthy (Rieff, *Mind* 47) can be interpreted as a variation of Skoda's use of autopsy results for diagnoses. "Through the study of the pathological," Paul Roazen has written, "Freud aimed to discern the normal" (*Freud and His Followers* 124). Freud's view of medicaments was also securely within the mold of the therapeutic skeptics. To Joseph Wortis he remarked: "a disease that can cure itself can be cured by medicine too, that is a general rule: medicine is an aid to the natural forces" (138). This view of nature was, as seen in Chapter One, a remnant of the influence of *Naturphilosophie* on medicine, one which the skeptics themselves retained. Worbs has argued that Freud actually came to medicine via *Naturphilosophie*, attracted by the influence of Schelling's philosophy on the essay "Die Natur," often attributed to Goethe. Just as likely, however, was Imre Hermann's proposition that the essay attracted Freud by virtue of its attribution of maternal qualities to nature (78). The most penetrating argument concerning Freud's initial decision to become a scientist was put forward by Schröter. He submitted that Freud's decision was an attempt at reconciling determinism and metaphysics. Schröter believed that Freud became aware of an internal struggle between these forces in 1873. The intelligence Freud had already shown would make plausible a profound understanding of that to which he wanted to devote his energies, and the possibility that he already recognized the most fruitful approach to the human mind, one which incorporated science and humanistic psychology. The story of Freud basing a major decision on a response to the reading of an essay had all the earmarks for Schröter of an anecdote (149). Especially Freud's statement that he heard the essay "just before I left school" (*Autobiographical Study* 14) lends further credence to Schröter's objection.

Another connection between Freud and his forebears at the medical school was his insistence on using the "scientific method as an investigating standard." This claim will be disputed below in a discussion concerning Freud's later works, but Roazen continued his remarks by anticipating such criticism: "when [Freud] speculated he was aware of it; he knew when a theory had been confirmed, and when it was still open to verification" (*Freud: Political and Social Thought* 117).

Indeed, Roazen concurred with Johnston in placing Freud within the tradition of the Second Viennese School, especially in regard to his giving priority to theory over praxis. Roazen cited a letter from 1912: "the therapeutic point of view . . . is certainly not the only one for which psychoanalysis claims interest, nor is it the most important" (*Freud and His Followers* 147). Freud's view darkened with time, especially with his discovery of the death impulse, as Bettelheim and Isbister observed (32; 240). Yet the latter author traced Freud's doubts back to the 1890s, at which time Freud frequently complained about his lack of success (240). In his last works, according to Ellenberger, Freud conjectured that in the future psychoanalysis would be valued much more as a science of the unconscious than as a mode of therapy (520), a conclusion which should not have upset Freud from what we have seen. Perhaps these very doubts about the therapeutic efficacy of his science inclined Freud to an aspect of therapeutic nihilism. "With time," Roazen wrote, "he came to feel that the cure of the besetting symptoms was not as important as understanding the underlying process" (*Freud and His Followers* 129).

At the same time the bringing of unconscious material to consciousness was Freud's idea of cure (Rieff, *Mind* 69; Wortis 64) so that, as Roazen noted, understanding and cure almost coincided in Freud's view (*Followers* 131). Perhaps this was in Roazen's mind when he posited in *Freud and His Followers* that as a clinician Freud was . . . a meliorist as well as a scientist" (247), a statement with which Rieff agreed (*Mind* 68). "Meliorist" was an odd word choice. The term, denoting one who believes in a world that is ever-improving because of man's efforts, seems impossible to reconcile with determinism, and no one has questioned Jones' conclusion that Freud "never abandoned determinism for teleology" (1, 50). Most likely both Rieff and Roazen intended the term in a narrow sense to describe Freud's "prescriptions for health, when health is in order . . ." (Rieff, *Mind* 68).

But more pertinent to the concern of this chapter is the question of determinism in Freud's view of civilization. For the psychoanalyst, civilization was based upon renunciation of impulses (*Civilization and Its Discontents* 44). Ten years before Freud wrote "his most important treatise on society" (Bettelheim 98–99; Jones 3, 364), *Civilization and Its Discontents* (1930), he had speculated that psychical processes and, indeed, life itself down to the cellular level, was dominated by a struggle between the life impulses (Eros) and death impulses (*Beyond the Pleasure Principle* 43). That Freud should trace human impulses back to protozoa is reminiscent of Rokitansky, who followed what he considered the fundamental motivating forces, hunger and movement, back to unicellular creatures.

Freud's postulation of a death impulse was predicated upon his observation of a compulsion to repeat, a tendency, he wrote in *Beyond,* that "recalls from the past experiences which include no possibility of pleasure" (14). Hence, Freud concluded in the same essay, "there really does exist in the mind a compulsion to repeat which overrides the pleasure principle" (16). This led Freud to view impulses as "conservative" forces rather than as drives toward change and development; to submit that *"an impulse is an urge inherent in organic life to restore an earlier state of things"* (30, Freud's emphasis). Only the sexual impulses were excepted from Freud's generalization (35): otherwise all impulses fell into the category of "ego" or "death" impulses which sought a return to the inanimate state from which life evolved.

The duality established by Freud in *Beyond the Pleasure Principle* was useful to him in explaining a phenomenon like sadism. How could the "sadistic impulse, whose aim it was to injure the object, be derived from Eros, the preserver of life?" Freud could now reply that sadism was a death impulse which had been repulsed from the ego and turned upon the love-object and had consequently entered "the service of the sexual function"

(*Beyond* 48). The postulation of a death impulse was also strongly supported by "the dominating tendencies of mental life," which according to Freud was "the effort to reduce, to keep constant, or to remove internal tension due to stimuli" (49–50). Freud reiterated rather more clearly and extended his theory of two classes of impulses in *The Ego and the Id* of 1923. To the class of death impulses he here added the "impulse of destruction directed against the external world." The drive to destroy was a partial expression of the death impulse (31).

Freud again looked to sadism, now described as the fusion of both classes of impulses, as the most persuasive argument for the existence of forces not subsumable within the category of sexual impulses. This followed a discussion in which Freud approached the conclusion that the impulses could all be derived from Eros after all. He wrote: "if it were not for the considerations put forward in *Beyond the Pleasure Principle* and ultimately for the sadistic constituents which have attached themselves to Eros, we should have difficulty in holding to our fundamental dualistic point of view." We can observe from this that the death impulses were fewer and less significant than the power of the sexual impulses, or as Freud expressed it, "the clamour of life proceeds for the most part from Eros" (36).

Freud's fundamental premise in Chapter Two of *Civilization and Its Discontents* mitigated the optimistic, though in reality neutral, tenor of the priority of Eros. "Life, as we find it," he submitted, "is too hard for us; it brings us too many pains, disappointments, and impossible tasks. In order to bear it we cannot dispense with palliative measures" (22). Life was a constant struggle. We strove for happiness impulsively: "the purpose of life is simply the programme of the pleasure principle," but our course was "at loggerheads with the whole world." Happiness was by definition a transient phenomenon for Freud: "we are so made that we can derive intense enjoyment only from a contrast and very little from a state of things" (23). While our very natures made happiness difficult to attain, its converse was readily available.

Suffering threatened the human being from no less than three directions according to Freud. Our bodies, "doomed to decay and dissolution," sent up their warnings by way of pain and anxiety. The external world was also ready to inflict suffering: nature "may rage against us with overwhelming and merciless forces of destruction." Finally, life in human society was capable of providing an unhappiness that struck us, due to its ostensible gratuitousness, as most painful of all. Yet Freud insisted that suffering caused by our fellow humans "cannot be any less fatefully inevitable than the suffering which comes from elsewhere" (24).

There followed, in the tradition of Schopenhauer and Rokitansky, the conclusion that "men are accustomed to moderate their claims to happiness — if a man thinks himself happy merely to have escaped unhappiness or to have survived his suffering" (24). Happiness then had become merely an absence of pain rather than the presence of pleasure. Further, like Rokitansky, Freud defined humans as basically aggressive. In "The Solidarity of All Animal Life" the pathologist had maintained that the satisfaction of conflicting goals required all organisms, including man, to be aggressive, and that indeed the very nature of all animal life was aggression (21). Freud echoed this view in *Civilization:* "men are not gentle creatures . . . they are . . . creatures among whose impulsive endowment is to be reckoned a powerful share of aggressiveness." Aggression for Freud was a deflection outward of the death impulse: "the inclination to aggression is an original, self-subsisting impulsive disposition in man" (69). We will see shortly that the connection between the death instinct and aggressive tendencies is tenuous.

In *Civilization* Freud differed with Rokitansky concerning the possibility of a way out of humankind's suffering. For the pathologist *Mitleid,* compassion, offered the hope of transcending one's egoism and penetrating another's ("Solidarity" 27). The psychoanalyst rejected that possibility: "No matter how much we may shrink with horror from certain situations . . . it is nevertheless impossible for us to feel our way into such people [great sufferers] . . . Moreover, in the case of the most extreme possibility of suffering, special mental protective devices are brought into operation" (36). Even more radical, Freud rejected the notion of loving one's neighbor altogether. He ruthlessly considered the statement from several vantage points: one's love was something special to those upon whom it was bestowed, how could one cheapen it by making it general? ; it would impose duties upon one impossible to fulfill in every case; but more importantly, "this stranger [is] in general unworthy of my love . . . he has more claim to my hostility and even my hatred. He seems not to have the least trace of love for me and shows me not the slightest consideration. If it will do him any good he has no hesitation in injuring me" (57). In Freud's world, man, neighbor or not, was constantly near the point of venting his aggression.

Freud's rather low opinion of man led to a conclusion that man without or before the civilizing process was no better off. Man's freedom was indeed greater before civilization: both sexuality and aggression were unrestricted. Yet this liberty "had for the most part no value, since the individual was scarcely in a position to defend it" (42). From this Freud concluded that "civilized man has exchanged a portion of his possibilities of happiness for a portion of security" (62).

Loss of happiness was itself due to the "heightening sense of guilt" (81). The psychoanalyst implicitly agreed with the position expressed by Rokitansky in his essay on the solidarity of the animal world: the restraint of aggression did not eliminate or even diminish the phenomenon (24). Where aggression was introjected or internalized, Freud argued, "it is . . . sent back to where it came from . . . There it is taken over by a portion of the ego, which sets itself against the rest of the ego as super-ego." Precisely the "tension between the harsh super-ego and ego that is subjected to it, is called by us the sense of guilt" (70). One need only have had the intention of being aggressive to evoke guilt feelings; "since nothing could be hidden from the super-ego," there was no psychic distinction between desire and fulfillment (72). The sense of guilt, which was the "most important problem" for civilization's progress, was simultaneously the cause of our loss of happiness (81).

This conflict between human happiness and civilization had

been foreshadowed in the first two chapters of Freud's *The Future of an Illusion*, written in 1927. In these pages are to be found perhaps the psychoanalyst's bluntest statements concerning humanity. He argued first that civilization had to be "defended against the individual" (3). Yet as the masses were lazy and unintelligent, "it was only through the influence of individuals that progress [could] be made" (6).

Again in *Future* Freud noted the destructive "trends" in men (5). This "psychological fact" signified that the true job of civilization lay not in taming nature for the purpose of acquiring wealth or even in the equitable distribution of wealth already obtained. "The decisive question," Freud wrote, "is whether and to what extent it is possible to lessen the burden of the instinctual sacrifices imposed on men" (5).

At the present time coercion was required to enforce renunciation of instinctual gratification for "men are not spontaneously fond of work and . . . arguments are of no avail against their passions" (6). Nor was the outlook for change very bright for a civilization without coercion: unswerving and disinterested leaders were required to serve as educators, "and it may be alarming to think of the enormous amount of coercion that will inevitably be required before those intentions can be carried out" (7). For Freud a great victory would be won if the majority that is hostile to civilization were diminished to the minority — perhaps that is all that could be accomplished (8).

Clearly Freud held out no great hopes for either man or civilization in the late works so far discussed. Jones submitted that "Freud always wrote in a vein of tempered optimism" and then proceeded by citing an example that undercut his contention. Freud noted that "changes will be carried out in our civilization so that it becomes more satisfying to our needs." Yet this hopefulness is demolished by the fundamental pessimism of the continuation: "but perhaps we shall also accustom ourselves to the idea that there are certain difficulties inherent in the very nature of culture which will not yield to any efforts of reform" (2, 366). Rieff's contention was that "far from being a residual idea left over from his biological training . . . Freud's theory of instinct [sic] is the basis for his insight into the painful snare in which nature and culture, individual and society, are forever fixed" (*Mind* 35).

Yet it is also possible to give Freud's postulation of the death impulse a neutral or even positive construction. Richard Rubenstein in his review of books by Earl A. Grollman and David Bakan observed that in *Beyond the Pleasure Principle* Freud had made of death a "Promised Land," much as the Jewish mystics had in their time. "We never cease yearning for its shores from the moment of birth," Rubenstein wrote. Thus Freud's death impulse, according to the theologian, was in itself not terrible: it represented the urge to return to the nothingness from which we began (44). Indeed Paul E. Stepansky has cogently argued that there was no logical link between an impulse that "wishes only to return" and man's desire to destroy, that is, between Thanatos and aggression (19). Freud's correlation of the two forces (*Civilization* 8, n. 1), Stepansky continued, was a rationalization allowing him to bear the horrors of World War I (161). Aggression was no longer a choice or random. Yet on Stepansky's argument Freud's view of man becomes even more fundamentally deterministic and pessimistic.

Max Schur, whose biography of his erstwhile patient Freud, centered around the psychoanalyst's relation to death, also provided a personal explanation for Freud's enunciation of the death instinct. Uncovering the urge both biological and psychological to die, to return to peaceful oblivion, "permitted Freud literally to live with the reality of death." Schur continued: "the formulation of the death-instinct [sic] concept – paradoxical as this may seem . . . prepared him for his belief in the supremacy of the ego, of the intellect, of *Logos,* the only force with which he could face *Ananke.* It paved the way for *The Future of an Illusion . . .* and for the formulation of a 'scientific' Weltanschauung" (332).

At the same time Freud's postulation of the conflict between Eros and the death impulse has brought him severe rebuke from several quarters. Freud's disclaimer that *Beyond the Pleasure Principle* represented "a far-flung speculation" (18) was not sufficient apparently to enable him as the founder of a science to indulge in his predilection for thinking aloud. According to Hannah S. Decker, Freud "was regarded by many physicians and psychologists as a throwback to the days of *Naturphilosophie* . . . Freud dared to give universal explanations . . . Freud's writing style cast discredit upon his conclusions because he did not limit himself to the dispassionate presentation of facts" (323). We saw that Freud's ambivalent opinion of psychoanalysis as therapy could be viewed, along with his ideas concerning medicine and the priority of theory over praxis, as remnants of therapeutic skepticism. Now in what were perceived as other prerequisites of correct scientific procedure: dispassionate objectivity and indeed rigid application of scientific method, Freud was found lacking.

Concerning the second of these charges, that regarding Freud's failure to employ the scientific method, Stepansky cited John Pratt's argument that Freud's contentions in *Beyond* were not "logically coherent [or] strongly based on empirical data." Rather, Stepansky submitted, Freud's theory of this duality relied on "dated theoretical biology." He continued, *"Beyond the Pleasure Principle* is clearly dominated by the then current vitalist conception, and the Eros-Thanatos theory that emerges is consequently nonempirical and vitalist, i.e., metaphysical-transcendental" (8). This is an interesting charge considering Freud's training within the Helmholtz School of materialism. Yet we have cited Freud's own position in "The Question of Lay-Analysis" that current materialist education was inadequate for psychoanalysts. And further there was disagreement concerning the role of materialism in Freud's outlook.

Frank J. Sulloway was the first to question the intensity and priority of the materialism with which Freud was confronted in Brücke's laboratory. In *Freud. Biologist of the Mind* he posited that: "by the time Freud began his medical training in the 1870s, the 1847 biophysics program had been in manifest retreat for many years. Indeed, by the 1870s, most of the movement's original members had frankly acknowledged the prematurity of their initial vision" (66). Ellenberger observed the same characteristic among the materialists that was noted by detractors of Freud's impulse theory as cited by Decker. The materialists, Ellenberger wrote, "produced vast speculative constructions, which . . . were nothing but the late resurgence of the philosophy of nature" (535). Yet Jones insisted that Freud "in his early student days . . . passed through a phase of radical materialism" (1, 402), a view with which both McGrath and Bernfeld concurred (99; "Freud's Earliest Theories" 355). Jones and McGrath were also in partial accord as to the cause of the mellowing of Freud's materialism: his attendance at lectures of philosopher Franz Brentano (Jones 1, 402; McGrath 111). McGrath cited Freud in a letter from April 1875 to friend Eduard Silberstein in which he referred to himself as a "former materialist" (98). Rieff implied that the severance of Freud's friendship with Fliess had great effect: Freud was cut off from his last immediate source of materialist counsel (5).

Whatever the time frame involved, one may fairly refer to Freud's approach to religion as materialistic in the sense that, as in discussing free will, Freud always insisted on tracing religious experiences to their psychic roots. In *The Future of an Illusion* Freud flatly refused to grant religion special consideration: it too must allow itself to be examined and judged by the rules of reason (43). As early as 1907 Freud was drawing the analogy between obsessional neurosis and religion. Roazen commented that "we have in this early essay ["Obsessive Acts and Religious Practices"] the nucleus of Freud's approach to religion. Religion is treated as an outcome of human needs" (*Freud: Political and Social Thought* 131). By the same token the "oceanic feeling" described by French novelist Romain Rolland in a letter to Freud of December 5, 1927 is presented as the persistence of his original ego-feeling, which has not distinguished the ego from the external world (*Civilization* 12–13). Analogously, when an American physician wrote to Freud that after having lost religious faith upon seeing a naked old woman in the dissecting room "God made it clear to my soul that the Bible was his Word, that the teachings about Jesus Christ were true, and that Jesus was our only hope," Freud mailed a "polite" response: "saying I was glad [he was] able to retain his faith. As for myself, God had not done so much for me. He had never allowed me to hear a voice, and if . . . he did not make haste, it would not be my fault if I remained to the end of my life . . .'an infidel Jew'" (Rieff, *Freud: Character and Culture* 271). The sight of the nude corpse had triggered a resurgence of the physician's Oedipus complex, Freud explained, and as his "ideas of 'father' and 'God' had not yet become widely separated," he could express his wish to destroy his father as doubt in the existence of God (272). Like the Oedipus complex itself, this doubt then "succumbed to a powerful opposing current." Freud concluded: "The conflict seems to have been unfolded in the form of a hallucinatory psychosis: inner voices were heard which uttered warnings against resistance to God. But the outcome of the struggle was displayed once again in the sphere of religion and it was of a kind predetermined by the fate of the Oedipus complex: complete submission to the will of God the Father" (273). This "religious experience," as Freud entitled his essay, was given the same treatment as Rolland's "oceanic feeling": both were explicated along psychoanalytic lines and interpreted as psychic disturbances.

Dividing Freud's conception of religion from his theory of civilization was purely arbitrary. Both religion and civilization evolved from the same primal setting, the one described by Freud in *Totem and Taboo.* Edwin Wallace discussed in some detail the prominent role of Freud's anthropological foray of 1912 in his subsequent sociocultural thought. Many of the ideas concerning instinctual life and its vicissitudes within civilization, spoken of in *Civilization,* can be traced to the much earlier *Totem.*

It was in *Totem* that Freud enunciated his elaboration of the Darwinian theory of the primal horde. This famous Freudian construction was based on a combination of the psychoanalytic interpretation of the totem with the totem celebration and the Darwinian hypothesis of the primal state of human society (*Totem* 915). For Freud the totem animal "is really a substitute for the father," who in Darwin's model, according to Freud, had been "violent" and "jealous," keeping all the females for himself (915).

One day the brothers of the horde joined together, rose up in rebellion, slew the father and ate his corpse. "Together," Freud observed, "they dared and accomplished what would have remained impossible for them singly" (915). This realization on the parts of primal brothers was the foundation of civilization. Simultaneously the brothers' ambivalent feelings towards their father, which included love, evoked a sense of guilt for their deed. After the murder "the suppressed tender impulses had to assert themselves [and] . . . the dead now became stronger than the living had been" (916–917). The sons reinstated the father's prohibitions and "undid their deed by declaiming that the killing of the father substitute, the totem, was not allowed" (917) except at annual totemic festivals. So as Rubenstein stated, "they were compelled both to confess their guilt and repeat the crime in the central religious act of the totem sacrifice" ("Freud and Judaism" 41). Totemic religion was based upon the brothers' sense of guilt, and further, all later religions proved to be attempts to solve the same problem" (*Totem* 918).

Freud traced the origins of both society and religion back to this primal murder, following which the former was "based on complicity in the common crime [while] religion [was founded] on the sense of guilt and the consequent remorse" (919). In his conclusion Freud verbalized what had already become quite evident: the development of civilization and its concomitants actually followed the psychic evolution of the individual. And quite specifically "the beginnings of religion, ethics, society, and art meet in the Oedipus complex" 927).

This portrait of religion or, in Rubenstein's argument, Freud's "myth of religion" ("Freud and Judaism" 41) is central to much of Freud's thought. Roazen correctly defined Freud's technique in *Totem* as being "channeled by [his] . . . attempt to apply clinical psychoanalysis as he had already developed it rather than to reconstruct it in the light of various religious systems" (*Freud: Thought* 135). This was clearly Freud's posture concerning religion throughout his career – one of the great tasks the psychoanalyst set himself was to explain religious belief psychoanalytically.

No one has denied the special place of Judaism in Freud's thought and personality, though the psychoanalyst himself spent little time on this or on any autobiographical detail for that matter. Concerns such as religion were considered private by Freud, as will be seen again below. We might find in this attitude a carryover from the therapeutic skeptics' rigid separation of profession from personal beliefs.

"My parents were Jews," Freud noted curtly in his *Autobiographical Study,* "and I have remained a Jew myself" (13). While at the University of Vienna, Freud continued, "I found that I was expected to feel myself inferior and an alien because I was a Jew. I refused absolutely to do the first" (14). The latter perceived expectation led to an important consequence: "I was made familiar with the fate of being in the Opposition . . . the foundations were thus laid for a certain degree of independence of judgment" (15). This sentiment was echoed in a citation given by Bakan. Freud advised Max Graf to raise his son as a Jew so he would "develop in him all the energy he will need for that struggle" (47).

These, Freud's only remarks about his religion and his response to anti-Semitism in his *Autobiographical Study,* are deceptively measured and calm. For it must he remembered that Freud to the end of his life gave a "presentation of himself as a 'godless medical man and empiricist,'" which McGrath submitted "was an accurate description of his *consciously* held philosophical position" (102). I have underscored "consciously" because, unlike Schnitzler, Freud actually had a turbulent relationship with religion. Philip Rieff in his *Freud: The Mind of the Moralist* offered a view shared by many readers of Freud: "It is on the subject of religion that the judicious clinician grows vehement and disputatious. Against no other strongpoint of repressive culture are the reductive weapons of psychoanalysis deployed in such open hostility. Freud's customary detachment fails him here" (281). There are two basic approaches to an explanation of the peculiarity alluded to by Rieff: one personal and the other professional. First there is good reason to see Freud's attitude to religion as his own attempt at reconciliation or accommodation with the tradition of his fathers, Judaism. Second, from the standpoint of his science, religion posed the most significant threat. The role of Judaism in Freud's personal life has been frequently discussed and in some depth. Most recently William J. McGrath has written at length (26–58) about Freud's religious background and particularly concerning the Bible Freud read as a child. This was *Die Israelitische Bibel* (1858) edited by Ludwig Philippson, which was, according to Spector, "a product of liberal Jewish scholarship and contained not only footnotes with a rational-scientific intention [but also] numerous woodcut illustrations . . . from Christian masters such as Raphael" (6). Freud had written in his *Autobiographical Study* that his "early familiarity with the Bible story . . . had . . . an enduring effect upon the direction of my interest" (14). McGrath perceptively noted that this was one of the few sentences added by Freud in his 1935 revision of the *Study* and concluded that, as this was just a year after completing a draft of *Moses and Monotheism,* Freud probably had Moses in mind (26). McGrath also depicted the fascination that the great Biblical dream-interpreter, Joseph, had for Freud as well, arguing that Joseph ranked with Moses as an emotionally significant figure" (27–44). Further, Marthe Robert added Jacob to the list of Biblical patriarchs with whom Freud felt a kinship: Jacob, who at an advanced age was led out of his country by his children (*Moses and Oedipus* 38).

Yet it was to the Biblical figure of Moses that Freud turned his attention in the 1930s in order to produce *Moses and Monotheism,* published in final form in the year of his death, 1939. Marthe Robert has written that Freud's Moses study represented the fundamental notions of *Totem* applied to the particular case of the Jews (*Moses and Oedipus* 139). Edwin R. Wallace raised the interesting notion that *Moses* was the "final chapter of *Totem and Taboo*" (261, n. 7), the section Freud suppressed in writing: "I am under the influence of many strong motives which restrain me from the attempt to discuss the further development of religions . . ." (*Totem* 919).

In his *Moses* Freud again put murder at the center of his

story. First Freud advanced the argument that Moses was actually Egyptian. To the previously postulated thesis that the name was itself of Egyptian origin (meaning simply "son") Freud added that in other "exposure myths," into which category the story of Moses' birth fit, it was the second family which was the child's authentic one. In Moses' case, then, his Egyptian family was genuine (13). Freud continued by arguing that "if Moses were an Egyptian and if he transmitted to the Jews his own religion, then it was that of Ikhnaton, the Aton religion" (27). Yet, Jahwe was certainly a volcano-god, and Egypt had no volcanoes (39). Freud resolves this difficulty by following a suggestion of Ernst Sellin. We read that the Egyptian leader Moses "met a violent end in a rebellion of his stubborn and refractory people" (42), and that there existed a second Moses associated with Qadesh and a Yahwist religion (46–49).

As in *Totem* but now in specific form, future generations of Jews experienced the guilt first felt by the actual murderers. It is within the context of guilt feelings that Freud approached the topic of anti-Semitism. Freud interpreted Jesus as "he who was most guilty, the leader of the brother horde who had overpowered the Father," or at least his "successor" and "reincarnation" (110–111). This act of expiation allowed Christians to charge Jews with the murder of God. They would add, Freud continued, that "it is true we did the same thing but we *admitted* it and since then we have been purified" (114–115). Another deep-seated cause for anti-Semitism was "gentile resentment of repressive Jewish morality" (Rubenstein, "Freud" 41), by which Jews "marked off their aloof position" (*Moses* 116). Further, most Christians, Freud continued, had acquired their faith only recently and were sometimes forced to it. These have a "grudge" against their religion, which they project onto its source (117). Finally, Freud included three more obvious explanations for anti-Semitism. First, the Jews were a minority, and there was need for animosity against an outside minority if the masses were to feel solidarity. The Jews were somehow different, Freud maintained; they were not a foreign Asiatic race but were different all the same, though "sometimes it is hard to define in what respects." Lastly, Jews were stubborn; they "defy oppression and have survived countless persecutions" (116). A consideration of Freud's motives in writing *Moses* perhaps casts more light on his relationship to Judaism than the content of the work. We have stated that Freud's published statements concerning his religion were attempts at rational consideration, but there was within him intense emotional responses as well. Friedrich Heer wrote that "all his life Freud's awareness of his own Jewishness was in conflict with his questioning of Jewish existence" ("Freud the Viennese Jew" 6). Jones questioned how it was that Freud, approaching the end of his life, became engrossed in the varied aspects of religion. "It hardly needed the bitter experiences of anti-Semitism," he commented, "to awaken in Freud such questions as 'How did I come to be a Jew? ; what exactly is a Jew'? " (393). But the Englishman continued by postulating that indeed it was the great anti-Semitism of the 1930s that compelled Freud to write his *Moses* (394).

Others have speculated, not without sound arguments, that Freud had urgent unconscious reasons for penning his study and for maintaining the thesis advanced. Roazen noted in *Freud: Political and Social Thought* that "the confused sequence in this work gives us formal grounds for suspecting that Freud was not at one with his thesis" (168), and Freud himself admitted "inner misgivings" which had delayed publication (*Moses* 69).

Among the most detailed studies of Freud's connection with Judaism is David Bakan's speculative *Sigmund Freud and the Jewish Mystical Tradition* (1958). In light of what was written earlier in this chapter and the work, above all, of Peter Amacher and William J. McGrath, Bakan's contention that "the tradition of severe materialism of Brücke, Helmholtz, and the like . . . was certainly not one which [Freud] seemed to draw upon in any essential way for psychoanalysis" (10) is untenable. Harry Trosman in *Freud and the Imaginative World* dismissed Bakan rather too readily, while admitting the importance of considering even remotely possible influences (20–21). Bakan's case is impressive in support of his central tenet, that "Freud, consciously or unconsciously, secularized Jewish mysticism; and psychoanalysis can intelligently be viewed as such a secularization" (25). Bakan's contention has also met with criticism from Henri Ellenberger, Marthe Robert, and Peter Gay, who argued in common that Freud had no cognizance of the Jewish mystical tradition and moreover, as Robert stressed, that Freud's temperament resisted all forms of mysticism (Ellenberger 544; Robert, *Moses* 159, n. 1; Gay, *Freud the Godless Jew* 130–131). Of course the question of an unconscious influence is not affected by lack of direct contact or even of apparent temperamental incompatibility. The numerous parallels culled by Bakan combine to make a case of at least partial influence virtually indisputable.

Bakan's study offers a further insight into *Moses*. Freud's work cries out for an interpretation based upon historico-biographical criticism, for, unlike any other of Freud's later writings, he, by his self-conscious uncertainty, is present in these essays. Ellenberger contended that Bakan exaggerated "the intensity of anti-Semitism in Vienna in Freud's youth and mature years" (544), but hyperbole of Viennese anti-Semitism in the 1930s would be difficult.

Despite the glossing over of anti-Semitism's effect upon him, in the *Autobiographical Study* the effect of this prejudice on Freud's career as well as upon his outlook generally cannot be gainsaid. The psychoanalyst's confrontation with it led him to an angry conclusion very much in contrast to his cool, matter-of-fact statements in the *Study:* "that on the average, people truly are, by and large, wretched rabble" (*elendes Gesindel*) (Abel 31). McGrath gave much significance to the story told of Freud's father, related in *The Interpretation of Dreams*. Jakob's hat was knocked off his head by an anti-Semite who commanded him to leave the sidewalk. That Freud's father responded by meekly picking his hat up out of the mud was a great disillusionment for Sigmund (McGrath 60). Thereafter, according to McGrath, anti-Semitism and Freud's ambivalence towards his father were linked in a significant manner. In the same year that Freud abandoned the seduction theory (1897), in which fathers, including his own, "had to be accused of being perverse," Freud also joined the B'nai B'rith, one of whose functions was to fight anti-Semitism (Mc-Grath 212–213). McGrath also summarized the arguments concerning the effect, if any, of anti-Semitism upon Freud's professional advancement. His conclusion, based upon a seemingly impartial and accurate assessment of the varied interpretations was that "on the whole, the evidence . . . supports the view that anti-Semitism was not only subjectively important as a fear in Freud's mind, but also objectively important as a factor in delaying his promotion" (176, n. 76). That one should consider the almost certain, and perhaps central, role of anti-Semitism in the writing of *Moses,* begun during the civil war in Vienna (1934), seems beyond reproach.

Moses, Freud's "most intense expression of his concern with the problem of Judaism," according to Bakan, may be "understood as a desperate and brilliant attempt to ward off anti-Semitism" (151–152). Freud, by arguing for Moses' Egyptian heritage, was attempting, whether consciously or unconsciously, to inform gentiles that the rigid religion of the superego was not of Jewish but of Egyptian origin. There was no need to hold the Jews responsible for a repressive morality.

Further, Bakan contended that the murder of Moses was a personal fantasy of Freud: "it is Freud who wishes that Moses were murdered . . . he wishes that the current repressive and oppressive forces associated with the Mosaic image would be killed" (164). Freud's opposition to the Law-Giver can be traced back to an earlier essay, "The Moses of Michelangelo" (1914), the hero of which, as Robert noted, was Moses and not the artist (*Moses and Oedipus* 265). In that brief article Freud described his own response to the sculpture: "Sometimes I have crept cautiously out of the half-gloom of the interior as though I myself belonged to the mob upon whom his eye is turned—the mob which can hold fast no conviction, which has neither faith nor patience and which rejoices when it has regained its illusory idols" (Rieff, *Freud: Character and Culture* 82–83). At the same time Freud "continued to see himself as Moses" (McGrath 312).

Rubenstein explained that no contradiction was involved in this simultaneous murder-identification: "only by ridding himself and Jewry of the Old Moses could Freud become the New Moses" ("Freud and Judaism" 42). There can be little question that Freud's Jewish identity grew under persecution, or perhaps it was only that Freud expressed his Jewishness more openly in the 1930s. In the context of Bakan's thesis, with the actual advent of the Nazis, there was no longer any need to attempt to shield the new science from charges of being an outgrowth of the Kabbala. Rubenstein cited (41) an anecdote found in Jones' biography. Immediately after the Anschluss of Austria, the Board of the Vienna Psychoanalytic Society met and decided that the seat of that organization should be wherever Freud settled. Freud drew an analogy with the destruction of the Temple in Jerusalem by Emperor Titus, after which Rabbi Jochanan ben Sakkai "asked for permission to open a school at Jabnek for the study of the Torah." Freud continued, "we are going to do the same. We are, after all, used to persecution" (3, 236).

For Freud, as for Schnitzler, conversion was not a valid recourse, though Worbs remarked that to avoid the ceremony of a Jewish wedding, Freud had played with the idea himself (183). To Wortis, the psychoanalyst betrayed the same sentiments as Schnitzler. "A Jew ought not to get himself baptized," he told his American student, "because it is essentially dishonest, and the Christian religion is every bit as bad as the Jewish" (144). Unlike Schnitzler, as we will see, Freud regarded himself as a Jew, rather than as a German, as seen in the letter of May 8, 1932 to author Arnold Zweig (E. Freud 412). Peter Gay cited Freud's comment to George Sylvester Viereck in this regard: He had considered himself German, he told the American interviewer, "until I noticed the growth of anti-Semitic prejudice in Germany" (90).

The same letter to Zweig helps define Freud's ambivalence toward Zionism as well. He wrote: "Palestine has produced nothing but religious, sacred frenzies, presumptuous attempts to conquer the outer world of appearances by the inner world of wishful thinking . . . it is impossible to say how much of the life in that country we carry as heritage in our blood and nerves" (E. Freud 411–412). Marthe Robert, who interpreted Freud's response to Zionism as "rather positive," cited a letter from Freud to Israel Spanier Wechsler, in which he alluded to the newly founded University of Jerusalem as "esteemed and dear" to him (*Moses and Oedipus* 40).

Good reason exists to agree with Worbs' conclusion, however, that Freud, like Schnitzler again, was rather more opposed to the idea of a Jewish homeland than otherwise (182). There is, of course, the public disclaimer, in Freud's Introduction to the Hebrew edition of *Totem*, in which he stated "that he could not espouse the Jewish nationalistic idea" (Ellenberger 463). More revealing yet was Freud's association of Theodor Herzl, the premier advocate of Zionism, with Moses. McGrath, in an unusual lapse, wrote that, despite the fact that "Freud's own attitude towards Moses always had a positive character, his view of Herzl as Moses seems strikingly negative" (314). McGrath did not employ Bakan's analysis, or this phenomenon would come as no surprise. There was, behind it, not simply, as McGrath noted, the competition of "a different approach to the world of phantasy" (314), but, as we have seen, Freud's ambivalence to the Biblical Law-Giver as well.

What has been examined here, Freud's motivations for penning *Moses,* is clearly an attempt at understanding the private side of the man. Freud seems to have filed the nonrationalistic aspects of his existence into the nonpublic category. For example, Freud, like Schnitzler, was fascinated by the possibilities of telepathy. When Jones informed him of the sensation his interest was causing in the British press, Freud replied (3/7/26): "when anyone adduces my fall into sin, just answer him calmly that conversion to telepathy is my private affair like my Jewishness, my passion for smoking and many other things" (Jones 3, 423). Freud equated his public life with psychoanalysis ("the whole content of my life") and with science (*Autobiographical Study* 136). This served as justification for excluding any merely personal experience that did not bear upon the founding or practice of Freud's science.

The essential opposition of science and religion was expressed in *The Future of an Illusion,* and in Chapter Thirty-Five of the *New Introductory Lectures.* These works represent Freud the scientist, the public Freud, attacking a competing world-view. As Roazen observed, religious systems tried to explain the same phenomena as Freud: "religious beliefs were a form of collective mastery of the unknown" (*Thought* 51). It is possible that Freud's rationalistic approach to religion derived from his liberal Jewish upbringing, as Percival Bailey (91) and Erich Fromm (*Mission* 3) have contended. Or, and this is just as tentative, Freud's rationalism could stem from his medical school training, from the emphasis on investigation and examination rekindled at, and enforced by, members of the Second Viennese Medical School.

Freud insisted in *Future* that religion had to submit to rational examination: "there is no appeal to a court higher than that of reason," he wrote (43). Upon investigation, belief in God revealed itself to be a means of exorcising "the terrors of nature," of reconciling men to the inevitability of death, and of compensating men for the "sufferings and privations which a civilized life in common has imposed on them" (24). Religion created a world which, contrary to experience, was righteous, where good was rewarded and evil punished, at least ultimately (26).

In its promise of equitability, religion offered a needed response to the sense of helplessness wrought by injustice (25). And when ancient polytheism gave way to monotheism, it became possible to "recover the intimacy and intensity of the child's relation to his father" (27). Despite the allure religion might possess, Frend argued that there were only two *rational* arguments for accepting religion: it was the faith of one's ancestors, and proofs existed from primeval times. He disposed of these points without much effort: our ancestors were more ignorant than we, and their "proofs" were "full of contradictions, revision, and falsifications." There was, finally, the super-rational argument— one was forbidden to raise the question of validity altogether (39–40). Such a claim was simply dismissed by the scientist; religion must be open to rational consideration.

Freud then described religion as an illusion, which he defined as a wish-fulfilling belief (49). As such, religion could neither be proved nor refuted, and Freud submitted that civilization would be better off without religion (57): indeed, man would naturally outgrow the need for it (71). The moral code needed to be secularized (68), and mankind needed an education to reality (81), by which Freud meant the acceptance of this world "warts and all."

There was an inherent optimism to Freud's argument in *Future*. Man was capable of rising above infantilism (81), and there was hope for a day when the intellect would be the highest power. The battle of instinct against intellect continued unabated, of course. "We may insist as often as we like that man's intellect is powerless in comparison with his instinctual life, and we may be right in this." But, Freud continued, in one of his most moving expressions, "there is something peculiar about this weakness. The voice of the intellect is a soft one, but it does not rest till it has gained a hearing. Finally, after a countless succession of rebuffs, it succeeds" (87).

Both in *Future* and in Chapter Thirty-Five of the new lecture series (1932), Freud contended that science held the only possibility for progress: "scientific work is the only road which can lead us to knowledge of reality outside ourselves" (*Future* 50). In his discussion of *Weltanschauung* near the end of his new lectures, Freud insisted that psychoanalysis could not be a worldview, but was, rather, subsumed by that of science. Opposed to the scientific *Weltanschauung* were those of art, philosophy, and religion, but only the latter was "to be taken seriously as an enemy." The argument against religion was the same as in *Future*, and included the evolution of religion presented in *Totem*. Religion, Freud concluded, was not able to stand up to critical examination. It had been shown by psychoanalysis to have "originated in the helplessness of children" (166–167).

It is interesting to observe that science did not actually qualify for Freud's conception of a *Weltanschauung*, which was defined as "an intellectual construction which solves all the problems of our existence uniformly on the basis of one overriding hypothesis, which, accordingly, leaves no question un-answered and in which everything that interests us finds its fixed place" (158). Freud here conceived of science as an ongoing process of discovery, limited "to what is at the moment knowable" (159). Possibly, he had in mind the scientific approach itself, as taught at the Second Viennese Medical School: everything was open to thorough examination; nothing was to be accepted without evidence. Had not Freud actually come back to his medical school training when he wrote that "there are no sources of knowledge of the universe other than the intellectual working-over of carefully scrutinized observations—in other words, what we call research" (159)?

Freud attempted to make clear that psychoanalysis was a discrete discipline. Bruno Bettelheim took pains to depict the founder of psychoanalysis as a great humanist, arguing that English translations were mired in Freud's "early stage," in which he "inclined toward science and medicine" (30). Without disputing the claim that Freud be considered a humanist, the discussion concerning science in the two works just examined are both late, and both glorify the scientific method, so Bettelheim was not precise either. Freud seems to have outgrown medicine, but not science. Put in words relevant to our context, we arrive at observations already made: Freud's materialism (for him represented by medicine) faded (Jones 1, 402; McGrath 111), but he never veered from determinism (science) (Jones 1, 50).

Freud saw his creation as existing apart from both medicine and religion. Bettelheim cited a letter of Freud, to the Reverend Oskar Pfister, referring to "The Question of Lay-Analysis" and *Future*. "'I do not know if you have guessed the hidden link between [the two],' he wrote, 'in [*Question*] I want to protect analysis from physicians, in the [other] from priests. I want to entrust it to a profession that doesn't yet exist, a profession of secular ministers of souls, who don't have to be physicians and must not be priests'" (35). Freud wanted to exclude the two extremes, the radical materialists being produced by medical schools, and the believers in miracles, who sought to transcend the determinism of science.

Determinist he was, as Wallace stated, both in his private and professional life ("Freud as Ethicist" 123), but despite the rationalist approach of his attacks upon religion, Freud was no pure skeptic. Once he had postulated the Oedipus complex (1897) as the centerpiece of psychic life, and other indispensable factors like infantile sexuality, Freud refused to question them. Indeed, consideration of other issues; religion, for example, was based solely on the psychoanalytic approach, and interpreted on the basis of psychoanalytic assumptions. According to Jones, Freud employed Lamarckian biology (inheritance of acquired characteristics) in arguing for the transmission of guilt through generations, even though he was well aware that Lamarck had been refuted (3, 335). Jones wondered why Freud did so. The answer is plain: Lamarck worked well with psychoanalytical theory. On the basis of Freud's abiding interest in telepathy, Roazen posited that within Freud there was also "the strain of the believer . . . This active, questing, anti-rational part of Freud's mind has been underplayed" (*Thought* 113).

Due to the complexity of Freud's personality, and the expanse of his education and productivity, he is frequently interpreted as the bridge over two cultural traditions. Marthe Robert understood Freud as having incorporated classical and Jewish culture, the former with effort, the latter intuitively (*Moses und Oedipus* 59). Freud, in this, was the model of an assimilated European Jew (50). Another quite popular assessment of Freud is as a synthesis of Enlightenment rationalism and the "dreamer and poet" of the Romantic "dark night of the soul" (Drucker, 97). This is the Freud who loved to read eighteenth-century rationalists and nineteenth-century depictions of the dream/reality dualism (Spector 8).

Yet the juxtaposition of this chapter with the preceding one brings to the surface still another significant tension within Freud, or perhaps even a key to understanding the paradoxical nature of much of his writing. Discussions of his output, as we have seen, often involved the very questions being debated at the University of Vienna Medical School prior to and contemporaneous with

Freud's attendance there: issues such as materialism and therapeutic expectations. For example, we have seen Stepansky charge
Freud with embracing vitalism in *Beyond the Pleasure Principle*
(8). Vitalism, belief in the existence of an inexplicable life-force,
had been the position of anatomist Josef Hyrtl at the medical
school, while Freud's early materialism was probably inspired by
the physiologist Ernst von Brücke, Hyrtl's arch-enemy. Not only
did we see that Freud's discussion of psychoanalysis' therapeutic
possibilities was within the context of the debate at his school,
centering around Rokitansky and Oppolzer, but Freud's tremendous faith in science, late in his career, as seen in *The Future of an
Illusion,* was also a throwback to the program of the therapeutic
skeptics. To a large degree, then, Freud's work was characterized
by the tensions that existed at the school that provided his medical training.

CHAPTER THREE

Arthur Schnitzler, Skeptic and Determinist

As was the case with Freud, a discussion of the relevance of the University of Vienna Medical School to Arthur Schnitzler's *Weltanschauung* must be filtered through the author's opinion of the school and of medicine in general. To an even greater extent than Freud's, Schnitzler's attitude toward the discipline and the profession was ambivalent, as evidenced in his autobiographical as well as in his prose and theatrical works.

To say medicine was in the Schnitzler family is no exaggeration. The author's father, Johann, was a renowned laryngologist. Arthur's maternal grandfather was a physician, as was Marcus Hajek, the man Schnitzler's sister, Gisela, married. Finally, Arthur's brother, Julius, was a noted surgeon. Medicine proved to be other than Arthur had dreamed as a child, as he described in his autobiography, *Jugend in Wien:* "like Papa, one would have . . . the possibility of riding around in the carriage all day [and] stopping at every confectioner" (90). Yet, one searches in vain for the foundation of Kupper and Rollman-Branch's assertion that, "Schnitzler entered medical school under bitter protest" (112). Rather, Schnitzler wrote in his autobiography, the example of his father, and the entire atmosphere of his home operated so as to preclude any other profession (90).

Schnitzler studied medicine from 1879 to 1885. Diary entries from this period, which was also the time of his first nonmedical publication (the poem, "Liebeslied der Ballerine," appeared November 13, 1880 in *Der freie Landesbote,* Munich), reflect a conflict between the two possibilities. As early as October 27, 1879, Schnitzler confided to his journal that he felt science would never come to mean as much to him as art already did. The diaries evidence that Schnitzler was not merely taken by aestheticism; rather, like Freud, he wanted fame, and, perhaps, perceiving qualities in his father and later in his brother which he lacked, he realized that literature might be the only avenue for renown. After citing the qualities of his medical relatives in his diary, Schnitzler observed that he could never be their equal and would return to his scribbling (*Schriftstellerei*) (9/20/88). Whereas Freud decided upon a medical career to keep his speculative nature in check and in that way win fame, Schnitzler did not want to curb his imaginative capabilities, for in them he perceived his hope for glory.

On January 2, 1880 Schnitzler expressed the fear of becoming a mediocre doctor, a threat all the more likely to occur because of his inability to study intensively. Both his diaries and autobiography are replete with descriptions of a disinterest in study that border on the humorous. At the same time, as the entry for December 15, 1880 reveals, the future playwright recognized the impossibility of his pursuit of both art and medicine.

Yet Schnitzler seems to have raced in both directions during his medical training. Just as the precedence of his publications went to a medical work, "Von Amsterdam nach Ymuiden" (Lederer 270), so too the majority of his attention and concentration, despite his reluctance to admit the fact, must have gone to medicine. The result: in 1885 Schnitzler received the equivalent of a Doctor of Medicine degree at the expense of having published almost nothing and having written quite little. Even his journal entries for 1881 and 1882 betray a unique irregularity, probably owing to his preparation for the *Rigorosa* exams, following which, he wrote of life becoming livable again (n.d., 1882, prior to 2/15). In his autobiography Schnitzler seemed intent upon preserving the image of a courtier's *sprezzatura:* "After I have narrated so much about my negligence in the medical sphere that one might believe one were reading the story of a hopeless, squandering student, may I be the less reticent about having dutifully got through the first Rigorosum, in the course of the third year, just as several of my more industrious colleagues." His examiner in physiology was the "dreaded" Brücke, and Schnitzler thanks the physician's "lenient mood" for his passing grade *(Jugend in Wien* 135).

One, if not the greatest, of medicine's drawbacks for Schnitzler was its obvious tendency to aggravate his native hypochondria. In mid-1881 he wrote that it would be far healthier for him if he were not a doctor. It was depressing to know the extent of illnesses to which one was exposed (*Tagebuch* June 27, 1881). On November 13, 1882 Schnitzler lodged a similar complaint, adding that medicine nevertheless held him in thrall to the extent that it absorbed his time and especially thoughts and strangled all aesthetic inspirations at birth. He concluded that it was still more beautiful to write a novella than to amputate a leg. Yet in *Jugend in Wien* the author drew a distinction between his feelings concerning medicine as a discipline and as a profession: "Now as before I am thankful to medicine for having sharpened my gaze and clarified my perception – that I chose it as a career, above all else considering my hypochondriacal predisposition, I saw as a grievous and irreparable act of stupidity" (322).

The practice of medicine itself was interesting only to a small degree: the few things that interested him, Schnitzler confessed in his journal, interested the human, perhaps the poet, in him (12/22/82). In his autobiography the author was more specific concerning medicine's attraction, again in a rather cavalier fashion. Even the two areas of his greatest interest, nervous and mental diseases, appealed not in a medical way, but only as they were rooted in the poetic or belletristic (187).

However unsteady Schnitzler's relationship to medicine, he never totally abandoned his practice. Worbs wrote in *Nervenkunst* that "even as a well-known and prosperous author, he treated friends and literary colleagues and read medical works to keep current with scientific progress" (196). At the height of his literary career, in 1910, Schnitzler wrote of medicine as a beautiful and decent profession, as opposed to writing, especially when the latter was pursued as a profession (*Tagebuch* 3/22/10). Not only was he thankful to the discipline for sharpening his view; according to his wife, Olga, Schnitzler considered himself a scientist (*Naturforscher*) much more than a poet (47), an observation that finds support in the diary entry of November 7, 1897, in which Schnitzler recorded his self-examination as a weak artist but a very profound judge of human souls.

Although the medical faculty and its achievements were not given much credit in Schnitzler's autobiography, there is ample evidence that the author was impressed by elements of the school and by some of the faculty's work. Professor Moritz Benedikt, student of Rokitansky and Skoda, who supervised Schnitzler's work at Johann Schnitzler's *Poliklinik,* was "as learned as he was taken with himself" (194). Heinz Rieder confused father and son when he wrote of the profound effect Josef Hyrtl's anatomy text had upon its reader (95). Arthur gave no clue as to his impression of the anatomist's masterwork; rather, he commented that the book, given to him as a gift by his father, remained, at first, unread (*Jugend* 91).

But the psychiatry text of Theodor Meynert, for whom Schnitzler, like Freud, served as assistant for six months (November 1886 to April 1887), fared better. The young doctor reviewed both Meynert's *Klinische Vorlesungen über Psychiatrie,* and the previously discussed *Sammlung von populär-wissenschaftlichen Vorträgen* for Johann Schnitzler's periodical, the *Internationale klinische Rundschau,* in 1891. Both books were found by the young Schnitzler to be difficult, a particular fault in a work, like the *Sammlung,* intended for a general readership. Specifically, and this is noteworthy because of the parallel with Freud's relationship to Meynert, Schnitzler objected to Meynert's rejection of hypnosis. Laymen, he protested, would accept the psychiatrist's negative assessment based upon his reputation, and would remain impermeable to the still-accumulating evidence ("Rezension" of *Sammlung* 778). Schnitzler must have found Meynert's *Vorlesungen* credible; he reported reading them again in February 1913, while working on his story, "Flucht in die Finsternis" (*Tagebuch* 2/21/13).

Schnitzler was also impressed by Meynert's clinical expertise, as he wrote in *Jugend in Wien:* "He was a great scholar, an excellent diagnostician . . . [but] as a physician in the narrower sense, in personal intercourse with the sick, at least at the clinic, he wrested no admiration from me. As convincing as he was concerning the case of illness, his bearing with the sick struck me as sometimes cool, uncertain, if not, indeed, nervous" (260).

The author's opinion of Meynert is significant as a statement of his position in the controversy concerning therapeutic skepticism, that is, in the debate discussed in Chapter One pertaining to the role of the physician. Even regarding Meynert, however, Schnitzler's attitude was not simple. In the passage just cited, he was implicitly advocating the conception of physician as healer, rather than as scientist. His critique of Meynert continued, however, to include reference to the psychiatrist's habit of attempting to dissuade patients from their "fixe Idee." As a youth Schnitzler found these efforts to be most alienating. But writing as an adult, the author wondered if the student should not, rather, have been moved by the world-famous psychiatrist trying to bend the law of nature through sheer energy of his human will (*Jugend* 260–261). This retrospective assessment, written a generation later (1915–1918), not only displayed sympathy for Meynert, though his actions remained inexplicable; more significantly, Schnitzler's sentiments were symptomatic of a mellowing of his youthful determinism, a subject to be dealt with below.

The importance of medicine to Schnitzler is reflected in the prominent role of physicians in Schnitzler's casts of characters. Approximately one-third of both prose and drama works contains doctors, and the percentage rises to over one-half at the mid-point of his career (Alter 8). Schnitzler's doctors, those who are secondary characters, are matter-of-fact, portraying qualities often associated with Schnitzler himself. They are "urbane, witty, successful in their profession, aware of belonging to an elite, confident in their ideas on man, society and life, [and] prone to be skeptical" (Alter 10).

Heinz Politzer in his generally insightful essay, "Diagnose und Dichtung. Zum Werk Arthur Schnitzlers," went a step further. Schnitzler gave the doctor, psychologist, scientist, and moralist, at most, the role which the chorus in ancient Greek tragedy possessed. According to the critic, the physician "functions as the knowing witness to an inexorably absurd fate." Here Politzer was referring to Schnitzler's total oeuvre, and, indeed, cited Professor Bernhardi as a case in point: "he is simply the leader of the chorus, who, unaware himself as to how, is thrust onto center stage." Bernhardi, in Politzer's view, must by no means be regarded as the hero of the play (140). Unfortunately, Politzer did not go into detail at this point in his discussion. If Bernhardi is not the hero in a technical sense (OUD, 1, 895), he does possess a number of qualities required of a hero, and, as the play's title makes obvious, was intended as the focus of the audience's attention.

In Schnitzler's literary output, the role of the physician is nowhere more prominently examined than in *Professor Bernhardi* (1912), and nowhere is the connection to Schnitzler's own medical training more direct. Moreover, the play constitutes a comprehensive analysis of a delicate ethical situation, as well as a discussion of a favorite Schnitzlerian topic, free will. The core of the plot consists of an encounter between Bernhardi, director of a medical clinic, and a priest, Franz Reder (literally, "talker"). The latter has been called by a nurse with the casual consent of a medical resident, Hochroitzpointner, to administer extreme unction. The dying patient is a victim of sepsis caused by a "forbidden operation," apparently an abortion (129). However, Bernhardi had just examined the girl, and though her condition remained hopeless, found her in a camphor-induced state of euphoria. Father Reder insists that she must not die without the sacrament, but Bernhardi refuses the priest entry on the grounds that his appearance would likely end what was, perhaps, "the happiest hour of her life" (134). When the clergyman persists, Bernhardi continues to bar his entry, arguing that "among my duties [as physician], when nothing else remains in my power, is the procurement of a happy death for my patient" (146–147).

The situation is a very difficult one. Bernhardi finally forbids the priest access to the patient on the authority that he, as physician, has been entrusted with the girl's well-being "until the last hour" (147). Of course, if the father's claim concerning the necessity of the last rites were accurate, Bernhardi's action in deterring the priest goes well beyond affecting his patient's last hour. In the event, however, Schnitzler has undercut, in a stage direction, the relevance of Bernhardi's interference. The clergyman had said, in an early response to Bernhardi's criticism, that perhaps the patient might be made ready for his visit. There followed the direction that the nurse, "unobserved by Bernhardi, upon a barely noticeable wink from the father, proceeds to the sickroom" (146). And, indeed, the patient dies almost immediately upon hearing of the priest's presence (148). Despite Bernhardi's best efforts, then, his patient is lost — indeed is lost without his immediate awareness.

This case of sepsis is central to the action of the play, and, as the plague of Albert Camus' novel of that title, is a synecdoche of the central theme of the work as well. For the sepsis (from the Greek "to rot" or "to make rotten") of contemporary Austrian society is also incurable, though again in this instance Bernhardi does what he believes best to save the "patient." We can find in *Professor Bernhardi* the literary counterpart of Schnitzler's assessment of Meynert, a judgment which bears the earmark of the therapeutic optimism of Johann von Oppolzer: the good doctor must try to help, though the case be hopeless.

The play begins with a reference to the large number of autopsies performed in Bernhardi's clinic, the Elisabethinum: clearly the influence of Rokitansky and Skoda was still felt. Indeed, the neurologist, Cyprian, presents himself as an assistant of Skoda (144), and as having worked in Brücke's laboratory (143). The connection with the University of Vienna Medical School is further manifested in the philosophy of several of the staff members of the clinic.

Another case, briefly discussed before that of the sepsis, involved a death from a kidney tumor. The autopsy revealed that Bernhardi had been correct in his diagnosis that the malignancy had not spread (133). Surgery, though unlikely to have helped, was not performed, based upon the decision of the professor of surgery, Dr. Ebenwald (130). It is made quite evident that Ebenwald misdiagnosed the case, but the aspiring resident Hochroitzpointner tries to ease his wounded pride:

> There would no longer have been any point in operating in any case.
> EBENWALD. Out of the question. Those over there at the Hospital can afford to perform such experiments, but we ... You know, dear colleague, internists are always in favor of operating in such cases. At the same time they feel we always operate too often. (133)

Here Ebenwald is employing an argument of the therapeutic skeptics (the inefficacy of much surgery) merely to shield his diagnostic incompetence. This lack of skill on the surgeon's part leads Dr. Adler (literally: "eagle"), like Rokitansky a pathological anatomist, to the following, possibly sarcastic remark concerning the surgical staff: "your main strength lies in diagnosis, not so much in therapy. Although you do experiment around a damned lot." One of Bernhardi's assistants replies that one must try new remedies when the old ones no longer work. Adler's response might have been spoken by any member of the school of therapeutic skepticism: "And tomorrow the new is again the old. You can't help it. I had to go through that myself once. But it is disquieting sometimes, that we have to grope around in the dark like that. Indeed, that was the reason I fled to pathological anatomy. There one is, so to speak, the chief supervisor" (141). Because the pathologist represents the school of therapeutic nihilism, tracing Schnitzler's treatment of Dr. Adler, though he is only a minor character, reveals something of the author's attitude to that philosophy.

The description of Adler's physical appearance is consistent with his name's meaning in German. He is small, black-haired, fresh, lively, with glowing eyes and a dueling scar (138). In German the word eagle has the same connotations as in English, mainly, keenness of vision and perspicacity. That he works long and hard is made clear immediately when he informs Dr. Cyprian that he is in the autopsy room until midnight (143). His perception of the role of the pathological anatomist, as evidenced in his remarks above, reflects a need for certainty, a goal which Adler does not, and perhaps cannot, attain.

Like Rokitansky, the weapon Adler chooses in his battle for certitude is objectivity. It is no coincidence that he is half Jewish, as though unable to judge, on the basis of available evidence, which religion is "correct." Indeed, Adler appears not to be a believer at all. When Bernhardi's assistant maintains, in response to Adler's contention that a pathological anatomist is the chief supervisor, that there is even a higher authority, Adler replies: "but he has no time to worry about us. He is far too occupied with another Faculty" (141).

In numerous cases the anatomist strives for impartiality. He admires the Jewish Bernhardi because of his success in an anti-Semitic society (142), and supports the promotion of assistant Dr. Wenger, also a Jew, because he is the better qualified candidate. Yet, Adler is the first to express, openly, his disapproval of Bernhardi's treatment of the priest (148).

The incident with Father Reder alters Bernhardi's career. Heads of the various staffs of the Elisabethinum meet to discuss the matter. During the session, the report is received that an official investigation will be undertaken into the charge that Bernhardi provoked a religious disturbance. Bernhardi's supporters are outraged when, as a result of the news, Dr. Ebenwald, the vice-director, demands a vote concerning the suspension of Bernhardi as director. For the only moment in the play Adler is very excited (*sehr erregt*), but his response is measured. He will offer his eye-witness account at any investigation, "but precisely because in my deepest soul I am convinced of Professor Bernhardi's innocence, indeed can testify to it," he believes an investigation should be made, so that "this matter can be clarified in an orderly manner before the entire public" (200). Despite his rose-colored assessment of an investigation, which avoids any consideration of stigma, Adler apparently does not think that a doctor under investigation should be director of the Elisabethinum, so he supports the motion to suspend Bernhardi, adding that his position is proof of his trust in the director (201).

Adler's *forte* is a logical consistency. While first Bernhardi, and then his supporters, Cyprian, Pflugfelder, and Löwenstein leave the meeting in protest, Adler remains, remarking to Bernhardi: "I would be unhappy if you misconstrued my behavior. At this time, it is incumbent upon me to express before all those present my especial respect for you" (206). At this point, as at their next meeting, Bernhardi responds with a Biblical reference which, in the context, approaches melodrama: "My best thanks. Who is not with me is against me" (206). Again, after Bernhardi's trial, at which he was sentenced to two months imprisonment, Bernhardi welcomes Adler to his home with: "A repentant sinner is more pleasing to my countenance than ten just ones." Adler responds lightly, "I was never a sinner . . . I stress again that this trial appeared to me from the very beginning as a necessity." He could not foresee, Adler continues, that the court would give more credence to Hochroitzpointner's version of the case than to his and Professor Cyprian's (214). The court had proceeded without the objectivity Adler claims he expected of it.

Bernhardi's last two responses to Adler must strike the audience as excessive. Much earlier, he had agreed to write an "explanation" of the entire controversy, saying that he had no desire to play the hero at any price (165). His overreaction to Adler is a response to the anatomist's lack of passion, perhaps, even, his lack of emotion altogether. But Schnitzler is not so judgmental in his portrayal of Adler. The anatomist is consistent, except for his support of Bernhardi's suspension, and a part of this consistency is his desire to be open, clearly understood, and fair—hardly negative traits. Still, Adler insists, pedantically, on having positive knowledge before acting—that was why he had turned to dealing with corpses. Bernhardi, on the contrary, sees correct action as being equally important as accurate perception (Rey, *Bernhardi* 56).

Schnitzler's sympathies were obviously with Bernhardi, who is despite weaknesses "a human among marionettes" (Urbach, *Schnitzler* 91). For the author's medical characters, both in *Professor Bernhardi* and elsewhere, Bernhardi served as the "ideal" rather than as a typical example (Alter, 11). Truly, he does not understand completely the implications of his actions, as Politzer argued (140), but he acts, and this willingness to work with less than total knowledge is attractive, if not philosophically sound or logically consistent.

Martin Swales wrote that "however much one may admire his integrity, there is clearly something morally inadequate about his total disregard of the social and political world" (60). William Rey saw this same quality in a different light. He argued that Bernhardi possesses a holistic approach to life, where inner and outer world, experience and feeling, intellect and inspiration are not antitheses, but coexist in a sensible connection (Rey, *Professor Bernhardi* 56). Both critics were correct: Professor Bernhardi may be sympathetic for the very "inadequacy" of his morality. Bernhardi appears to be willing, as Rey noted, to pay the price for his individualism (58), for his benign disregard of social expectation. Morality, in the sense intended by Swales, is simply societal regulation.

Professor Bernhardi cannot be termed a true rebel because his "rebellion" is unintended. For Politzer, Bernhardi's ignorance of how he came to be the center of a maelstrom seemed to preclude the possibility of Bernhardi's heroism. But Maria Alter offered a valid, contrary view: "Bernhardi's superiority rests on both expected and surprising attitudes: altruism, self-assurance, and a deep conviction that one may violate a socially consecrated practice if it contradicts a subjective interpretation of humanitarian values" (11). Despite Bernhardi's efforts, however, the society to which he returns from jail is shown in a "precisely so questionable light . . . as in the beginning" (Rey, *Bernhardi* 82). Perhaps this lack of improvement was what led Politzer to conclude that Bernhardi was not a hero.

The obvious approach to the end of *Professor Bernhardi* would be to view it as an example of therapeutic nihilism justified by the fact that, in spite of best efforts, the sepsis remained. Rey captured well the brutal reality of the play's conclusion: "Justice is . . . unrealizable, truth falls a sacrifice to the powers that be" (*Bernhardi* 82).

Only by looking to the individual, to Professor Bernhardi, could one find possible affirmation of the world in Schnitzler's play. Though Schnitzler was not severe in his portrayal of the clinically objective Adler, any optimism arising from the play derives from Bernhardi and his example. Maria Alter was correct in her summary of Schnitzler's physician. Yet, concerning *Professor Bernhardi,* her conclusion applies mainly to the protagonist alone. She wrote that Schnitzler's physician was: "above all a free individual who shuns both social systems and systems of ideas, and is motivated by an authentic interest in other men. His inner light does not proceed from principles, but from a professional activity that involves his fellow man. In short, his rebelliousness and his sense of mission are both grounded and expressed in his *praxis,* in the very best anticipation of existentialism" (19–20). It is noteworthy but not atypical of Schnitzler that, while he clearly sympathized with the concerned physician, with the therapeutic optimist in terms of the discussion in Chapter One, he did not condemn the representative of the opposing school. Indeed, one can interpret the lack of change or improvement wrought by Bernhardi's efforts as an example of therapeutic nihilism writ large.

The notion of human struggle is central to *Professor Bernhardi.* Beyond depicting Schnitzler's ideal physician, and the playwright's stance concerning therapeutics, the work is part of Schnitzler's lifelong meditation upon the question of determinism and human freedom. Even as an eighteen-year-old, he posed the question of whether a person's formative influence was already exhibited at the moment of coitus. Were intellectual (*geistige*) directions dependent on the speed of sperm, or on the spiritual or physical condition of the procreators? The youth offered no reply but rather recognized the incomprehensibility of his musings (*Tagebuch* 4/28/80).

By the time of *Professor Bernhardi*'s première, Schnitzler's approach was more sophisticated. In barring the priest entrance to the sickroom, Bernhardi has acted on the basis of his personal perception of a physician's duty. Swales accurately delineated the ethical question in the work, when he wrote that "it would seem . . . there are two standards of morality involved: one is that of instinctive, spontaneous humanity which gives an inward certainty of right and wrong, the other is the morality of the social organization . . ." (59). The critic found fault with Bernhardi for acting upon the first of those standards, but there is no evidence in the play that Schnitzler shared Swales' qualms.

The ethics of two social organizations are particularly contrasted with Bernhardi's subjective morality: those of the government bureaucracy, and those of the Church. The former is represented in the character of Professor Dr. Flint, who has recently been elevated to the post of minister of education. He and Bernhardi had been medical school colleagues, which makes his betrayal in a speech to Parliament (198) all the more callous. He had taken Bernhardi's part and had pledged to defend him. Yet, while speaking, Flint's keen sense of his audience's expectations compelled him to alter his course. The politician's vacillation, in response to unrest in the Parliament, is exquisitely portrayed by an eyewitness: "Then the minister somehow deviated from his theme, became angered, so it seemed, and confused. Then somehow he came to the necessity of religious education, to the connection between the Christian world-view and the progress of science . . ." (198). Flint ended his speech, "to his own surprise," we are told, by agreeing to support an investigation into Bernhardi's "religious disturbance" (198). This flexibility on the part of the bureaucrat is not anything new: Bernhardi reminds Flint of a medical school experience which the latter had conveniently forgotten. As a resident, Flint had refused to offer a diagnosis of which he was certain because it contradicted that of his chief. The indirect result of his reticence was the death of the patient.

Flint defends himself in both instances by recourse to the argument of ends justifying means. Ambition had not been his motive. In the case of withholding his diagnosis, Flint argues, the "sacrifice" of one life had to be made "for the good of the hundreds of other human lives which were later entrusted to my medical art" (173). Similarly, his reversal in Parliament evokes the following defense: "But ultimately – you have to understand, there is something higher in public life than keeping one's word" (245). The very same proposition is put forth by the priest. He comes to inform Bernhardi, following the latter's sentencing, that he believes the physician had acted in the only way appropriate to his profession. Bernhardi asks the obvious question: why had the priest not made a statement to that effect to the court? Like Flint, for whom the growing unrest of members of parliament had uncovered a new necessity, the priest had had a breakthrough, which came with the "force of divine enlightenment." He had realized in court that by speaking he could hurt the object holiest to him. In the exchange that follows Bernhardi again reveals his straightforward manner in ethical questions, while the priest appeals to a greater good:

> BERNHARDI. I just cannot think that for a brave man like Your Reverence, there could be a holier thing than the truth.
> PRIEST. What? Nothing holier ... than the paltry truth ... You yourself would not even contend that. Had I ... publicly acknowledged your right to keep me from the bed of one dying, a Christian, a sinner, then the enemies of our Holy Church would have exploited such a declaration beyond measure .... (221)

The priest is as presumptuous as the minister of education: both believe they can forecast the response of others, and take action to prevent the assumed result.

Schnitzler undercut the criticism of Bernhardi's subjective morality by having the ethically questionable Flint present it. Clearly the education minister is neither sympathetic nor particularly intelligent. Yet his accusation that Bernhardi frequently, "in the certainly noble excitement of the second," lacks the ability to take in the broad perspective (175) is accurate and approaches the criticism of Swales (60). More is involved, however, in Bernhardi's actions, as he recognizes. His final dialogue with the like-minded Hofrat Winkler argues against Politzer's thesis that Bernhardi merely finds himself at the center of controversy. At least, after two months incarceration Bernhardi explains that "the problem was no longer Austrian politics or politics in general; rather, it suddenly dealt with general ethical things, with responsibility and disclosure, and in the ultimate sense with the question of freedom of the will." The Hofrat responds cynically that all questions finally devolve to that point, if one insists on following them to their base. Better, he continues, to brake earlier, lest, one fine day, one begin to understand and forgive everything. And where would be the appeal of life if one could no longer love and hate? Bernhardi insists that one continues to love and hate regardless (252).

The thought being expressed is found more clearly stated among Schnitzler's aphorisms. One would think, Schnitzler wrote here, that a universal belief in the law of causality would lead to the elimination of emotions. All actions would be thought to have reasonable motivations. But, Schnitzler believed, the very nature of society, indeed, the instinct of self-preservation itself, would compel one to act as though one loved or hated (*Aphorismen und Betrachtungen* 32). Schnitzler was actually positing the paradoxical notion that existence *is* determined to the extent that it cannot allow for acceptance of total determinism. This significant paradox found an even more direct expression in a later entry: to the extent a determinist is convinced of the exclusive mastery of causality, he would be compelled to understand one believing in free will, "as this belief must signify a necessity for the determinist as well" (*Aphorismen* 249).

Schnitzler's attitudes toward determinism and materialism were not static. As a medical student, in the same year as, and perhaps in response to Meynert's essay dealing with the subject ("Über die Gefühle" 1880, *Sammlung* 67), Schnitzler addressed the question of materialism and determinism in his journal. For

Meynert, as we have seen, human freedom was an illusion or appearance which obtained only because science lacked the keys for unlocking the door of the brain's inner sanctum. Schnitzler, as an eighteen-year-old, accepted a good deal of his future instructor's argument at the expense of the anatomist Hyrtl. Schnitzler wrote that to his sorrow the materialist perspective was becoming ever more plausible, more probable. He viewed Hyrtl's efforts in discussing the anatomy of the brain as mere polemics, and continued by echoing Meynert's words. The time would come when the subjective part of ideation and consciousness would be explicable through the arrangement of cells. If this point were not reached, Schnitzler continued, the fault would lie in a failure to perfect the microscope. But even granting the refinement of the microscope, Schnitzler posited, one would never be able to answer the question of why certain arrangements of cells led to a person's superior imagination or memory. The furthest science would ever reach, the young author insisted, would be the ability to link certain mental constructions with special abilities: to be able to suggest, for example, that, if certain cells are round, one's intellect will turn to action. But further than that, Schnitzler exclaimed, science would never go (*Tagebuch* 4/28/80).

What the eighteen-year-old Schnitzler was leading to was the question of a first cause. Even if and when science were able to determine a configuration of neurons or a particular shape of cell that produced certain types of persons, the question of how the necessary positions or shapes came into existence would remain unanswered. Almost fifty years later, in *Der Geist im Wort und der Geist in der Tat,* Schnitzler expanded this question in addressing his typological diagrams. The language was more refined, but the author's position was virtually unchanged: "It is not improbable that mental composition (*Geistesverfassungen*) is tied to certain anatomical-histological relations. To a certain, hard to determine degree, this might apply to . . . specific talents . . . predispositions of character, temperament, characteristics which are very probably conditioned by physical-chemical, indeed, mostly inner secreting processes of a regular or changing nature . . ." (34–35).

Despite the materialist ring of the above, Schnitzler insisted that he was not attempting a materialist explanation for talent, for the condition of the soul, or constitution of the mind (*Geist*). Even if relationships between these and their physical correlations could be established, the actual essence (*Wesen*) of the mind and soul would be unintelligible as before (35). Knowing that the optical nerve allows sight, Schnitzler reasoned, did not explain the phenomenon of sight (35).

Yet one wonders at Schnitzler's entire enterprise. *Der Geist im Wort und der Geist in der Tat* is an attempt to classify types of intellectual constitutions, for example, poet, statesman, hero, or general. Schnitzler insisted the diagrams were not value-bound, but their construction, an upright triangle resting upon its reflection (a downward pointing triangle) makes value judgment inevitable. The poet is at the apex of the diamond entitled "Der Geist im Wort," while the man of letters (*Literat*) is at the nadir. Analogously, the hero tops the rhombus entitled "Der Geist in der Tat," with the swindler at its lowest point.

As Schnitzler is observing character types, predetermined by innate attributes, the categories are fixed. There can be no crossing of the center line joining the two halves of each diamond. Thus, not only can a swindler not become a hero, but a politician can never be a statesman. In the idealistic tradition of the Viennese Medical School discussed in regard to Freud, Schnitzler was here implying the existence of a noumenal world and the ultimate incapability of science to penetrate that world. Schnitzler stood in the determinist/materialist tradition insofar as he accepted a typology of human intelligence, and posited its predetermination based upon biological factors. Like the cat of Meynert's poem who drank the milk of weakness while lusting for blood, Schnitzler wrote that one can prevent a person from stealing but not from being a thief (*Aphorismen* 127). In both instances the fundamental nature of the animal could not be altered, only corrections could be made to allow for coexistence.

The inability of the materialist to supply the first cause despite his continual probing remained one of Schnitzler's main objections to the school of thought. In his journal entry for June 28, 1880 the author seemed to think he had found an answer. He described a friend's world-view as relying solely on the idea of force, while denying the role of matter, whose existence, in Schnitzler's opinion, was certain. Matter existed, and a force either from outside or within set it into movement. Nothing remained of this force as it became movement, or rather, it existed as movement, and it would always exist in that way. Schnitzler's youthful view was a reiteration of the introduction to Rokitansky's *Handbook of General Pathological Anatomy* published in 1846: "A correct view of force and matter teaches that there is not force without a material base . . . all appearances are subject to matter" (Neuburger, "Rokitansky als Vorkämpfer" 2).

Much later, in his aphorisms, Schnitzler questioned where precisely such reasoning led one. If, as is the case according to Schnitzler, the determinist grants that a miracle was the beginning of all things, what is that wonder other than God? And what exactly happened to that God? Regardless of whether He is here now or not, Schnitzler continued, He remains unintelligible (*unfaßbar*), remains a wonder (*Aphorismen* 31).

This view concerning a first cause led Schnitzler to the notion of free will, which, he argued in his aphorisms, is an extension of God. Can one really imagine a God who contented Himself simply with the creation of a law of causality? "No, He did not make things that easy for himself. He set an equally noble opponent in the universe, free will, who is ready, at any time, to take up the battle against causality" (*Aphorismen* 32).

Schnitzler seems to have traversed a great distance, from a youthful belief in a Helmholtzian world where "everything that happens is nothing but reciprocal action between matter and matter," and in which the ego itself "is also only a totally unessential indication of a certain thing-in-itself, namely, the organic being" (Lederer 277), to maintaining, as an adult, not only the existence of free will, but also a free will that was God's agent in man.

In Schnitzler's literary works one can perceive an analogous mitigation, though certainly not the elimination of determinist tendencies with the passing of time. "I write diagnoses," the playwright once observed, and though, as Worbs noted, Schnitzler was stamped by the empiricism of the modern doctor (197), there is in later works a movement away from a stark, clinical perspective. A good example of the author's dry objectivity is "Mein Freund Ypsilon: Aus den Papieren eines Arztes," which Schnitzler wrote in 1887, two years after completing medical school. The choice of name already reveals the central concerns of the story. Ypsilon, German for the letter "Y," is not only a means of maintaining anonymity (as, for example, the patient "Y"), and a mathematical term (the Y-axis), but is simultaneously the German word for a common moth, *Noctua gamma*. These three usages of "Ypsilon" correspond to science. Yet a fourth meaning, which will be discussed later, can be extrapolated from David Bakan's examination of Freud's *Interpretation of Dreams:* "the *Yod* (Y) often designates a Jew" (38).

The theme of "Ypsilon" is the proximity of creativity and madness. "Y"'s girl friend tells the narrator that "Y" "is . . . half a fool," to which the physician responds, "half a poet, so a total fool" (31). As in *Professor Bernhardi,* to name one of many examples, the doctor is unable to help, as both the narrator and Ypsilon realize long before the end. The doctor notes, "["Y"] looked at me smilingly, as though he wanted to say: 'you fool, do you really think that this should help me'"(34), a statement actually expressed by "Y" a page later.

Not surprisingly, the conclusion underscores the significance of Y's name. Like the "moth to the flame," the poet is drawn, inexorably, to insanity and death: "Moody, golden imagination! The one you approach flatteringly, in fragrant friendship, and mold him into that happiest of all fools, a poet; the other you raid like an enemy, and make him into the most pitiable of poets, a fool!" (39). The story's theme, as summarized in the conclusion, is both a fair example of Schnitzler's early penchant for determinism and, yet, serves as an interesting contrast to his medical instructors' view of art. For Ernst von Brücke, art represented, on one level, an inexplicable enterprise, a phenomenon for which the materialist world-view was inadequate. Schnitzler's dark portrayal of imagination goes beyond even the pessimistic analogy drawn by Meynert in his poen "Moos." There, the imagination, though paralleled with moss, was at least a positive factor in a bleak vision. For Schnitzler in "Ypsilon" the creative imagination is a *cul-de-sac* ending in insanity.

Two years after "Ypsilon" Schnitzler composed another tale with a first-person physician-narrator: "Der Sohn. Aus den Papieren eines Arztes." This very brief story is particularly significant here, for it served as the nucleus for Schnitzler's last work, the novel, *Therese.* "Der Sohn" is related by a doctor called to attend a dying woman. The woman, he is told, has been assaulted by her son, who, at the beginning is sitting apathetically across from her. She pleads with the physician to take her son's part after her death. In response to his questions she related that she had tried to kill her son immediately after birth. The rest of her life was spent attempting to compensate the boy for her crime and assuaging her guilt. Yet throughout she had felt his hatred.

What remains of the story are the doctor's ruminations concerning his own intervention. He resolves to speak to the authorities, "for, it seems to me, it is by far not clear how little we may want to, and how much we must [do]" (86). The physician is simply not certain that the mother was not correct in believing her brutal act shaped her son's personality: "Did not obliterated memories of the first hours of our existences remain with us, of which we could not think, but which did not disappear without a trace? " (86).

Although, by the very nature of the differing genres, the novel, *Therese,* involves additional characters and situations, its core is the same incident. And though told in the third-person by an unidentified narrator, *Therese* consciously shares the objective, case-history nature of "Der Sohn." In a diary entry for September 19, 1924 Schnitzler recorded completing a reading of "Der Sohn." He noted that there was much good in the story, and that it almost seemed worth the effort to work out and complete. The social note now interested him. In keeping with his apparent plan to emphasize the societal aspect of his tale, Schnitzler appropriately appended the subtitle "Chronik eines Frauenlebens," for the work is on the surface a listing of a succession of employment and romantic situations in the life of a not particularly noteworthy governess. Martin Swales' assessment was accurate. "Most of the characters," he wrote, "are . . . purely episodic in function; they appear briefly when they happen to cross Therese's path and are not seen again" (38).

One of the redeeming factors of the novel is Schnitzler's treatment of the core-story; in comparing, we see how the author's determinism had matured and gained in sophistication. For now we are presented not merely with murder as a *fait accompli,* as in "Der Sohn," but with a "before," "during," and "after" as well.

The story of the novel begins with the rather rapid mental deterioration of Therese's father, Lieutenant Colonel Hubert Fabiani. Not yet sixty, Fabiani had retired and moved his family from Vienna to Salzburg. Very shortly after the move Fabiani begins to display symptoms of paranoid schizophrenia: "delusions of grandeur," "loss of reality contact," and a general "disintegration of personality and intellect" (Weiss, "The Psychoses in the Works of Arthur Schnitzler" 386). Within approximately one year, the retired officer requires institutionalization.

Therese's mother is presented as an emotionless, often confused woman. She relates to her children the plots of the novels she has been reading, but in so muddled a way as to give the impression that she was blending the contents of various books together (8). Eventually she becomes a successful novelist. The mother-daughter relationship is encapsulated in chapter eighty-six, in which Therese is in need of money. Almost as one makes a decision in a dream, the narrator writes, Therese found herself on the road to her mother. "It was not longing, not the feeling of a long neglected duty that drove her there, rather, simply the fact that she knew no one else from whom she might borrow the money. . . ." Therese's mother is no less unsentimental. She is willing to lend her child the money, "without hesitation, almost . . .

in any case against a note of liability, with repayment required by
the first of November; failure to repay in a timely fashion would
entail an interest charge of two per cent per month" (210). This
businesslike arrangement is only one confirmation of an unhappy
relationship that has existed at least since Therese's sixteenth year
when the action of the novel begins.

When one adds to the equation the very loose connection
Therese has with her brother, Karl, one begins to apprehend what
Frederick J. Beharriell noted as the novel's "psychology of loneliness" ("Arthur Schnitzler's Range of Theme" 305, n. 22). Therese
is unhappy at school, where other students begin to avoid her
when rumors of her mother's nocturnal visitors begin to spread
(14–15). Her first boyfriend, appropriately named Alfred Nüll-
heim, though probably truly devoted to her, lacks spontaneity
(18) and seems incapable of emotion. Following a mutual visit to
Therese's father in the asylum, Alfred, who aspires to medical
school, speaks of the visit "without any sadness, more in a pleas-
antly aroused manner . . . and did not notice the tears . . . that ran
down her cheeks" (14). So it cannot surprise the reader when, as
Alfred is preparing to depart for medical school, Therese feels
nothing (19). But her relations with other men are no different: it
is not, as Beharriell submitted, "the author's attitude to the sex
act which is 'colorless' and 'mechanical,'" but how intercourse
must seem to Therese. Yet she is driven by her loneliness to seek
amours.

Therese's isolation is the motive for her response to Kasimir,
the man who fathers their son, Franz. She is in the Prater amuse-
ment park – it is spring, though the trees are still bare. They sit in
an inexpensive coffeehouse where Kasimir tries to entertain her.
She realizes that, though he is trying his best, he is not in the least
witty. Yet after long months, during which no one had spoken a
single harmless or humorous word to her, "in this constantly
oppressive atmosphere of constraint and seemliness," an incredible
longing had arisen in Therese for happiness. She thus finds herself
at the side of a person whom she had not known an hour ago,
thirsting for an opportunity to be a bit happy and to laugh (60).

Franz, who will bring Therese her greatest unhappiness before killing her, is ultimately a product of this urgent need to find some levity in a drab existence. The reader is given a clue that Therese's flight from her everyday gray life is doomed to end tragically: near the couple at the cafe sits a man in black suit and top hat — odd attire for a spring day (60).

The description above of Therese's encounter with Kasimir, with its motivation in alienation and its outcome seemingly predetermined, points to a social determinism. But even more significant in the transpiration of events are the hereditary factors involved in both Therese's personality and that of her son. Kasimir's seduction of Therese is another example of the novel's matter-of-fact sexual encounters. The narrator notes three details. One of the legs of the armchair into which Kasimir pulls Therese seems about to break off, and his mustache has the scent of mignonette pomade, "actually like a barber shop from which she, as a child, used to pick up her father." Finally, Kasimir's lips possess the unpassionate combination of attributes: "damp and cool" (66). All three of these observations, beyond characterizing a rather tawdry scene, point to the unfavorable outcome of the affair. Most noteworthy is the connection drawn between Kasimir and Therese's father, who has gone insane.

Kasimir does not display psychopathic traits of behavior; he is merely an unreliable, lying manipulator. Therese knows this side of his nature: "she knew that he lied . . . but even his lies belonged to him, yes, it was precisely they that made him so lovable and seductive" (84). Perhaps Therese's own very low self-image compels her to cling to a man she knows to be lacking in basic scruples. Thus, when after informing him of her pregnancy, Kasimir disappears, Therese's "shock was not as deep as she had expected: in her innermost self she had been prepared for the same" (86).

Some twenty years later, not long before she is murdered, Therese chances upon Kasimir playing cello in a cheap night club. Their glances meet more than once, and it becomes quite obvious that he does not recognize her (227). How little their relationship meant to Kasimir is underlined in an encounter a short while later.

Not unexpectedly we learn that Kasimir is a pseudonym, and he has forgotten Therese's name. He can barely conceal his lack of interest in the course her life took after their affair. Further, he reveals, quite accidentally, that he had been married and the father of a child when Therese had entered his life. Therese boards the train, and her smile quickly disappears. Schnitzler concludes the chapter with a brief but shattering description of Therese's loneliness. She looks back and "still watched as he turned and headed back. Snow fell softly and densely: the streets were void of people. And the man, who for so long had been Kasimir Tobisch, the father of her child, vanished from her, an anonymous one among anonymous others, and vanished forever" (254-255).

By supplying in some detail the personality of Franz's progenitors, Schnitzler offers an alternative explanation of a son's matricide to that provided in "Der Sohn." In *Therese* Franz is depicted as a conglomerate and exaggeration of flaws from both sides of his family. Interpreting Franz's act as an inevitable consummation of hereditary flaws gives no greater room for freedom of the will than the mother's elucidation in Schnitzler's short story.

Franz's personality flaws and crimes are legion. Robert O. Weiss, who described Franz as Schnitzler's "most meticulous picture of constitutional psychopathy," has made a list that includes "early criminal tendencies, lying, thievery, truancy, forgery, incorrigibility, dissolution, and promiscuity," among others. Weiss has included Franz in his chart of constitutional psychopaths for whom he provided no etiology for the disease, "because hereditary factors seem to play the most important role here" ("Psychoses" 392). These factors are more significant than social influences, for example, as evidenced by the fact that Franz spends the formative years of his life with a rural family which is, relative to the Fabianis, unremarkable.

Schnitzler, however, retains in *Therese* the plausible explanations for Franz's murder contained in "Der Sohn." The entire theme of Therese's (and the mother's) guilt is elaborated. In the novel Therese comes very close on several occasions to having an abortion, changing her mind at the very last moment. The birth scene reveals that she still lacks any maternal feeling for the child. Upon waking she looks at his face, and her first thought is that "he was no doubt dead. Certainly he was dead. And if he was not dead, he would die in the next seconds. And that was good" (96). The child does not respond to Therese's wishful thinking. She realizes he is quite alive, and his existence is sinister, even threatening (96). Her complex feelings about herself are reflected in her ruminations about Franz: "My child . . . And this child was an independent whole, a being existing completely for itself: possessed breath, blood, and a little voice . . . that still came from a new lively soul. He was her child. But she did not love him. Why did she not love him, as it was her child?" (96). The reason she does not love her child is precisely because he is hers. A short time later, in what operates retrospectively as an archly ironic statement, Therese says to the infant: "Come little child, come little Kasimir . . . you won't become so bad a man as your father, will you?" (97). Neither at this juncture nor later does Therese feel hatred for Kasimir. She does not reject the child because of his father.

Therese wishes both her child and herself dead. And, even as she contemplates his murder, she feels guilt for having wanted an abortion, that is, for having desired his death earlier. Then she apparently attempts to suffocate the child (97). It is noteworthy that the reader cannot be certain whether Therese actually attempts the murder or has merely dreamed the entire scene: we next read that she awakens, "as though from a terrible dream" (97). The description is not simply another example, so common in Schnitzler's œuvre, of the indistinguishability of dream and reality. Rather, the point Schnitzler makes is more specific and parallels Freud's, in his *Civilization and Its Discontents* (71) of two years later. Therese experiences a sense of guilt regardless of whether she actually attempted the crime or merely dreamed it. In his journal entry of January 3, 1922 Schnitzler had already foreshadowed this insight shared with Freud. There can be a feeling of guilt, he noted, without a bad conscience, and added parenthetically that this was perhaps the worst type.

When Therese recognizes that the baby is still alive: she brings it to her breast. Holding it fast, Therese thinks of the night she made love to Kasimir. That hour, she speculates, and this one: that night and this morning, that haze and this incomparable clarity, "did they really stand in some kind of connection? " (98). This question, along with the guilt Therese feels, are parallel to the question and emotion raised by the mother in "Der Sohn."

The mothers in both works feel that there is a causal link between their murderous thoughts and near-deeds, and the criminal development of their sons. On one occasion Therese looks at her son and in his glance perceives not just "obduracy, lack of insight and of love, but also bitterness, scorn, indeed a concealed reproach." His glance compels her to think back to the night of his birth, to the moment when she thought, actually wished, he had died (176). Yet in the novel Franz's glare might well have its antecedent in that of Therese's mother. Shortly before her father is committed, Therese notices her mother's glance: "meaner and more hateful than usual" (11).

And in the novel Schnitzler does not link Franz to Therese's father merely on the basis of the scent of Kasimir's pomade. When Therese asks her old friend Alfred, now a physician, his opinion of her son's condition, he uses the English term, "moral insanity" (189), the latter word of which could refer to Lieutenant Colonel Fabiani. But for Therese there can be only one explanation of her son's twisted life: "her heart resonated with compassion, and with complicity . . . complicity, yes, that is what it was . . . as though she alone, she who bore him, shared responsibility for everything he did . . ." (248).

The concluding scenes of the novel, like that of Franz's birth, are much more vivid than their short story models. Schnitzler parallels Franz's murder of Therese with her imagined or real attempt on his life: not only in its method, cutting off the air-supply but also in his response: " 'nothing's happened, mother,' he suddenly called. Her eyes were open. She blinked, she watched. No, she was not dead. Not much could have happened" (260). As in "Der Sohn," the mother (Therese) asks the physician

(Alfred) to provide the court with mitigating testimony for her son. For Therese, like her counterpart, sees Franz's act as just: indeed, Alfred notes, her lost son is turned in this transformation into the executor of eternal justice (262). Alfred fulfills Therese's wish, but his testimony fails in its intent. The State's attorney argues that Franz could not have had memories of his first hour of life, and that the introduction of such mystical tendencies could only obscure justice. The Court, however, does consider Franz's birth out of wedlock, and concomitant substandard upbringing, as mitigating circumstances (263). This ruling is based upon a notion of behaviorism – that Franz was shaped by his environment. Clearly, Schnitzler has been asking, throughout *Therese,* whether hereditary factors are not at the very least of equal importance to environmental ones. Moreover, as we have seen, though providing alternatives, he has not totally abandoned the trauma-at-birth motif of "Der Sohn." What the State's attorney condemns as mystical is quite concrete in Therese's psyche.

Another aspect of the debate between determinism and free will plays a large part in Schnitzler's last published story, "Flucht in die Finsternis" (1931). One also finds in this "complete picture of schizophrenia, paranoid type" (Weiss, "Psychoses" 381), three key elements of therapeutic skepticism: the attempt to explain disease from purely material causes, the lack of genuine concern for the patient on the part of the physician, and the ultimate inability of the doctor to aid the sick. Finally, the story is evidence of Schnitzler's own masterly comprehension of a mental disease and shows "perhaps most impressively among Schnitzler's works his outstanding qualities as a medical observer" (Weiss, "A Study of the Psychiatric Elements in Schnitzler's 'Flucht in die Finsternis'" 273).

Though published in the year of the author's death, notes for such a tale were made in 1909 (Rey, *Arthur Schnitzler. Die späte Prosa als Gipfel seines Schaffens* 155), and the story completed in 1917 (Weiss, "Psychiatric Elements" 381). This latter date is significant, for Emil Kraepelin had only recently introduced the notion of *dementia praecox,* and "even the most prominent psychiatrists still considered pure paranoia a common and distinct disease unit" (Weiss, "Elements" 381). Schnitzler's characterization of paranoid schizophrenia in the character of Robert must have derived in part from keen personal observation. Weiss listed no less than fifteen symptoms of paranoid schizophrenia displayed by Robert (Weiss, "Elements" 381), and Rey commented upon Schnitzler's avoidance of the Romantic glorification of insanity (*Prosa* 176). But "Flucht" is not only a clinical description of an insane man's fratricide and subsequent suicide. It was apparently Schnitzler's belief that, to a certain extent, one actually makes a conscious decision for either health or sickness. It is probably no coincidence that two aphorisms touching on this matter employ the word "Flucht," or the verbal form of the word, numerous times: "some flee to insanity as to death; and both could have been courage as well as cowardice" (49); and, "there exist all sorts of flight from responsibility; there is a flight into death, a flight into illness . . ." (44). Again, one can see a kinship to Freud, who had postulated a similar phenomenon in "The Question of Lay-Analysis" (136).

Robert's brother, Otto, a physician, appears to interpret Robert's illness in the light of a choice of eschewing responsibility. Otto informs his brother that he believes that behind the insane actions of many of the mentally ill are to be found "a tendency toward sour grapes, falsehood, buffoonery: in short, an indecent striving to shirk the true seriousness of life and uncomfortable responsibility" (166–167). His prescription for Robert's nervous disorder had been six months of unaccompanied, leisurely travel (129).

Robert, in fact, does not appear to possess any great ambition (136, 139, 141). Moreover, he has a different view of responsibility. While idly watching as his busy brother visits a patient, Robert speculates upon the difference of thought and deed. What differentiates, for example, a death wish from a murder? Robert reasons: "thoughts disappear, deeds are irrevocable." Significantly, he views this truth as the "spite of providence" and finds it unfair that one must live with one's deeds long after the emotions that compelled the acts have vanished (165).

Robert looks to his relationships with others to avoid responsibility: that is why he requires confirmation of his illness, and why he literally prays to his beloved, Paula. For a large part of responsibility is the willingness to stand alone. Walking home one night, Robert suddenly has the feeling of a "monstrous forsakenness": "and suddenly, a saving thought came to him, that Paula was in the world, and that he was no longer alone. Save me, he mumbled to himself . . . and he threw his glance up, as though the senseless insane thoughts had taken flight into the nocturnal heaven, back to nothingness" (173). If Robert's illness is more than acute loneliness, and it is, still, close companionship helps – it allows some escape from his own personality as well as from total responsibility for himself.

Like Otto, the other physician in "Flucht," Dr. Leinbach, does not believe in the reality of Robert's disease. He smiles when Robert expresses doubt in his ability to return to work, and when Robert protests against this reaction by observing that he already had to be sent away for six months, Leinbach responds: "my dear friend, if one is in the lucky situation of being able to be sent away, naturally we send him away. On the other hand, there are many people who simply lack the time to go mad" (136). When Robert complains that he still does not feel totally well, Leinbach prescribes a couple of days in the mountains, not from necessity, but as a contrast and a fitting close to Robert's trip (137).

Rather than merely lacking concern, both doctors are probably responding to what they perceive as Robert's hypochondria (131, 133). This phenomenon plays a basic role in the question of choice in illness. Clearly, one who only imagines himself ill would appear *prima facie* to be guilty of irresponsibility, yet Schnitzler is aware that true hypochondria is a disease itself (Scheible, *Arthur Schnitzler und die Aufklärung* 30–32). There some question about the difference between being ill and feeling that one is ill. Indeed, Walther Riese questioned whether, perhaps, "there is no basic difference between health and disease," and, whether psychoanalysts might not be correct in viewing the two as representing only a difference in degree ("History of Ideas in Psychotherapy" 455).

Ironically, it is Otto, later to fall victim to Robert acting upon his delusions, who draws a concrete distinction. In a conversation with his brother the physician separates those who respond physically to their hallucinations from those who do not (166). At this point in the narrative Robert falls into the latter category but by the story's conclusion he has joined the former. Schnitzler thereby reflects the difficulty or impossibility of anything more than a fleeting diagnosis.

In the concluding paragraph of the tale Dr. Leinbach brings forth these two points: he questions the reliability of established diagnoses and seems skeptical about the entire enterprise of separating disease from health. The narrator has reported that Robert's was considered an obvious case of persecution mania. Dr. Leinbach prefers to write that Robert suffered from the fixed idea that he was to be killed by his brother. Indeed, there proved to be some validity in Robert's fear: after all, he is found dead three days after killing Otto (209). Robert could not foresee exactly how his brother would cause his end but he had had a presentiment. "And what are presentiments?" asks Dr. Leinbach. "Only a sequence of ideas within the unconscious: the logic of the metaphysical, one might say." But medicine, Leinbach implies, requires a different classification; requires the use of a term with associations that had been studied: "We . . . talk of hallucinations! . . . as though this word . . . did not signify . . . a flight into the system from the quarrelsome diversity of the individual case" (208). As will become clear in the discussion of Schnitzler as a skeptic, the systematization of psychological phenomena was perhaps his greatest objection to Freud's new science. In the context of this story, employment of the term "flight" in describing medicine's tendency to classify disease has a particular bite. The word is used frequently and by the time of Leinbach's summation has come to mean a trip without destination (163, 193).

Schnitzler has included a number of elements in "Flucht" that defy the "system." Throughout the story the brothers' relationship is marked by strange intensity. The narrator, on the opening page of the work, enters Robert's consciousness and notes that though signs of it might be slight, both felt an inextinguishable connection to the other. In fact, of all possible relations in a man's life, Robert judges the fraternal as the only one that has a natural permanence, a belief that he himself will bring to a morbid fruition at the end of the tale.

From Robert's point of view brother Otto is ultimately best friend or archenemy. He assigns to his sibling great insight. Dr. Leinbach, Robert notes, could easily be swindled, "but Otto would not give one such an easy game . . ." (140). Because his tie with Otto is so strong it is not surprising that Robert begins to amalgamate their faces, and even their fates. First he transfers his suspicions of his own mental disorder to his brother (180). As his condition deteriorates the association becomes faster. While discussing the site of a mutual childhood experience Robert looks at his brother and "suddenly, with horror, he caught sight of a countenance that he recognized. It was the same one that had recently stared back at him from the mirror—his own . . ." (189). The ultimate expression of Robert's sense of identity with his brother is their shared death. Schnitzler precisely describes Robert's murder of Otto: he shoots his brother in the heart: but ingeniously omits any technical detail of the sick man's death. We are told only that his body was found three days later, some seven hours by foot from the town where he had killed Otto.

Even before this shared death, in which, again, Robert's individuality is blurred, he had written an outline of his life, in which he linked their fates inextricably: "awareness of my own complicity in my brother's delusion. Are we both perhaps manifestations of one and the same divine idea? One of us two must enter the dark" (201). The account continues with his prediction that Otto will go first, but after the idealistic identification of the two his own fate cannot be different.

Robert's difficulty with his identity is underscored by speculations concerning freedom versus necessity that run throughout "Flucht." There are indeed, as Rey observed, scenes that evoke

the impression that Robert's future is predetermined (*Prosa* 175).
A Lieutenant Höhnburg, friend to both brothers, fell victim to incurable insanity, much to Robert's surprise. As Robert thinks back
to the occasion at which his brother had predicted Höhnburg's
death, he reflects that this "perhaps secretly had announced his
own fate" (132).
The crux of the matter of freedom, in Robert's case, goes
back to the question of whether illness is a choice. As he is walking with his future fiancée, Paula, he wonders whether his life
might have been different had he known her earlier. Or, "was my
existence sketched from the beginning? Or, did I have the choice,
at some time, the choice between weakness and strength, between
health and being ill, between clarity and confusion? But, then, had
something already been decided?" (156). Yet in each case, and
this was overlooked by Rey, the reader is made privy to Robert's
thoughts, and not merely observations by the narrator. When
Robert reflects that as a youth he was considered a crank and even
as crazy (180), this is the past filtered through his consciousness.
Perhaps the point here is that, to cite the title of a play by Luigi
Pirandello, "it is so if you think it is so."
    Robert's self-deprecation and his willingness to view his life
as fated can be interpreted, as was his need for relationships, as an
expression of his irresponsibility. Schnitzler did not choose the
word "Flucht" simply for its alliterative qualities with "Finsternis." The word, meaning "flight" or "escape," connotes choice,
unlike, for example, the German "Fall, or "Sturz." And, indeed,
Robert recognized his choice but did not, or, and this is the unanswerable question, could not make it. One arrives, it seems, at
Dr. Leinbach's summary comment about the "quarrelsome multiplicity of the individual case" (208).
    What we have seen in looking at several of Schnitzler's works
is enough to cast doubt on his reputation as a rigid determinist.
Already at this point one might reject Claudio Magris' assessment
of Schnitzler, whose skeptical determinism, the critic maintained,
"conformed with the clinical glance of the physician, who views
feelings and passions as mechanical-physiological impulses reacting

like chemical elements . . ." (75). This description, which is quite precise for the case of Goethe's *Wahlverwandtschaften,* is totally refuted by Schnitzler's "Traumnovelle" of 1925. One imagines Freud would have worded his congratulatory letter of 1922 differently following a perusal of this work.

"Traumnovelle" is an exception in Schnitzler's oeuvre. Like Freud's comment and Magris' assessment, Janik and Toulmin's view of Schnitzler is valid only if one excludes this novella. The authors of *Wittgenstein's Vienna* see Schnitzler as mainly concerned with the difficulty of communication. People "cannot communicate, because they encapsulate themselves hopelessly within social roles which satisfy their immediate desires, and thereby rob themselves of all hope of more lasting fulfillment" (63). It is as though to disprove this charge that Schnitzler penned "Traumnovelle."

The story begins with a child reading a fairy tale aloud to her parents. Very early in the tale the wife, Albertine, asks her husband, Fridolin, to agree always to be frank (63). They have just related to each other romantic experiences not involving the other. At the end of the novella both have again exchanged the most intimate and possibly incriminating dream and dreamlike experiences, after which, "[they] lay . . . both silent . . . until, as every morning at seven o'clock, a rap at the door and a light child's laugh from next door began another day" (129).

Schnitzler's "Traumnovelle" treats marriage sympathetically but realistically. The marriage of Albertine and Fridolin, the everyday world of responsibility, and, by extension, the whole social fabric of our culture is shown to successfully resist the instinctual part of human experience. Rey provided a succinct summary: "What Schnitzler has fashioned here is nothing less than the preservation of marital love from the attack of the spiritual underworld. The nocturnal forces of Eros break into the world of day, of order and morality. The conscious sees itself threatened by the unconscious. In a time that preached the preponderance of the id over the ego, Schnitzler dared to give shape to his belief in the world of day" (*Späte Prosa* 99).

Both husband and wife have had unusually intense experiences. Albertine has had a dream in which a Dane, to whom she had been attracted, makes love to her, while her husband spurns the love of a princess and is crucified for his refusal. Albertine's response is a cruel, mocking laugh, which Fridolin hears upon entering their bedroom (100). He is shocked by her dream, and believes that at that moment he hates her more than he ever loved her (106). And yet the two have something even deeper. At the same time that Fridolin feels hatred for his wife, he realizes that he is still holding her hand, with an "unchanged but more painful trust," and he even kisses it tenderly. He thinks: "They lay next to each other, like mortal enemies. But these were just words" (106). There is a profounder communication than that of language.

Fridolin has had a dreamlike adventure himself. Called to treat a patient, he finds the man already expired. The man's daughter, though engaged to a history teacher, professes her love for him, but Fridolin does not respond (70). The physician is in no hurry to return home; he is upset over Albertine's admission that she had found the Dane, of whom she will later dream, attractive. Fridolin encounters a prostitute but ultimately refuses to sleep with her (76). He goes to a coffeehouse where he meets a former medical school colleague who helps him gain entry into what appears to be an orgy attended by members of a secret society.

Schnitzler makes quite clear that Fridolin's experience is not a dream, as when the next day, for example, Albertine discovers the mask her husband had worn to the orgy (127). And even the weird setting and costumes of the party can find their counterpart in Schnitzler's Vienna. Hartmut Scheible noted that the masquerade follows the lines of Stefan Zweig's description of fin-de-siècle Viennese bordellos, in his *Die Welt von Gestern*. It is not the form of the secret society that is fantastic, Scheible continued, so much as the need for such a meeting-place, created by the strict separation of private and public lives (*Arthur Schnitzler und die Aufklärung* 86–87).

Fridolin is discovered to be an outsider and faces an unknown, but certainly severe punishment. He is saved by one of the women, whom he presumes to be a whore, dressed as a nun. He had been strongly attracted to her, and now she is willing to suffer death for him. She takes his place, and he is compelled to leave. The next day, he reads of the death of a Baroness Dubieski (dubious?) by poisoning. He follows the leads he obtains and by midnight finds himself at the pathological anatomy institute hoping to identify the body of his savior.

Schnitzler spends a good deal of time on the scene in the morgue of Vienna's *Allgemeines Krankenhaus.* As in *Professor Bernhardi,* the pathologist's name is Dr. Adler, and it is interesting to speculate whether Schnitzler might have had the same character in mind, only ten or fifteen years older. In the play Adler informs Cyprian that he works until about midnight (143); in "Traum-novelle" the pathologist works during the night when he is free of disturbances (126). He answers Fridolin's knock brusquely, obviously unhappy at the interruption. Yet the Adler of "Traum-novelle" is a mellower man than his namesake and seems genuinely interested in his colleague's pursuit, asking him twice whether he has found the Baroness' corpse (124, 126), and laying his hand soothingly on Fridolin's arm (126).

One of the corpses, Fridolin believes, possibly could be the Baroness. He overcomes an initial revulsion and examines the body. Rey has written that, precisely because Schnitzler was a true physician, he could not be gruesome (*Prosa* 15), and the descrip-tion of a corpse bears out the critic's opinion. Fridolin holds up the face rather tenderly in both hands and is confronted with a pale countenance with half-closed eyes. "The lower mandible hung down slackly, the small, pulled up upper lip revealed the bluish flesh of the gum and a row of white teeth . . . it was a totally void, empty—it was a dead countenance" (124). Fridolin goes on to examine the body in detail. Full of compassion, he actually locks fingers with the dead woman. Schnitzler has combined tenderness with morbidity here and has captured the physical reality of death without being grisly. As in *Professor Bernhardi,* so here, as Rey concluded, the physician is "stamped with comprehension, co-passion, and goodness" (*Prosa* 15).

Immediately following this moving interlude Fridolin finds refuge, as throughout his adventure, in his profession. He pays close attention to Adler as the pathologist shows him a new staining technique (126). As was the case on his way to the secret orgy, as he was changing into his disguise, he "thought, as of something redeeming, that in a few hours . . . as every morning, he would go around the beds of his patients – a beneficent physician" (87). And before tracing his savior's whereabouts, Fridolin pursues his medical duties with alacrity (113) even though it has entered his consciousness, "that all this order, all this proportion, all this security of his existence were only appearance and lies" (113).

But as the ending of "Traumnovelle" makes apparent, the imposition of order through daily routine, through familial and professional responsibility, is the only means of defeating the dark instinctual world of humankind. It is made clear by Schnitzler, here as in *Therese,* that there is no actual distinction between dream and waking: both are parts of human psychical activity. Thus, Schnitzler draws a number of links between Albertine's dream and Fridolin's waking experiences: Albertine's would-be lover is a Dane, and the password to Fridolin's orgy is "Denmark." Religion is burlesqued in both encounters: at Fridolin's orgy, the whores are dressed as nuns, while in her dream, Albertine scornfully laughs at her husband's crucifixion. No wonder, then, that Fridolin's last words are, "and no dream . . . is fully a dream." Albertine's response, "now we are truly awakened" (128), indicates that she too has become aware of the relationship of the two sides of human life.

It is noteworthy that Schnitzler moved one step further in "Traumnovelle" than to posit the overlapping of dream and wakefulness. At about the same time that Freud composed *The Ego and the Id,* in which he discussed the idea of a pre-consciousness, Schnitzler's thoughts had alighted upon the same notion.

Schnitzler has Fridolin reflect about so-called *Doppelexistenzen,* who abruptly leave their accustomed parts of the world for varying lengths of time, then return without knowledge of their own whereabouts. In diluted form, the experience is more common, Fridolin continues: "For example, when one returns from dreaming[.] To be sure, one remembers . . . but certainly there are also dreams that one totally forgets, of which nothing remains but a certain puzzling mood, a secret giddiness. Or one remembers only later, and no longer knows whether something has been experienced or merely dreamt" (116–117). These memories of dreams were stored somewhere, just as information passing from consciousness to unconsciousness, and vice versa, required a part of the psyche. Both Schnitzler and Freud discussed this waiting area, as it were, of the human mind at about the same time. Freud, in *The Ego and the Id,* wrote: "'how does a thing become preconscious?' [on the way to becoming conscious] . . . the answer would be: 'through becoming connected with the word-presentations corresponding to it'" (10). Similarly, one reads Fridolin's analysis above, or Albertine's statement when her husband insists she complete the retelling of her dream: "It's not so easy . . . these things don't really allow themselves to be expressed in words" (103).

Schnitzler, Scheible has observed, already entertained the notion of a *Mittelbewußtsein* in his diary entry for March 9, 1915 (*Aufklärung* 102–103). With the passage of time, Schnitzler increasingly came to emphasize the importance of this area of the psyche. In 1926 he disputed the terminology of Freud's division of the psyche and put forth an alternative partition into conscious, mid-conscious and under-conscious, arguing that the second level had been both underrated and relatively unexplored. Indeed, this mid-section constituted "the most enormous area of spiritual and intellectual life: from here elements uninterruptedly rise to consciousness or sink down into the unconscious" ("Über Psychoanalyse" 283).

According to Francis Rolla, it was precisely here, on the ground of the mid- or pre-consciousness, that Schnitzler and Freud most closely approximated each other's thought. With the recognition of this new terrain, both rejected previous psychological explanations of literature. Schnitzler designated the new area, his so-called *Mittelbewußtsein,* as the field of poetic activity, whereas Freud situated artistic activity in the *Vorbewusstsein* (pre-consciousness) (Rolla 204–205). Of greatest importance here is that this intermediate area, called by either name, was captured in both instances from the unconscious terrain of the psyche. That is, the unconscious, as Freud now also recognized, was not to be granted so great a power as heretofore (Scheible, *Aufklärung* 104). A further contact with psychoanalytic thought helps illuminate Schnitzler's position concerning materialism/determinism. In a note dating from after 1908, Schnitzler implied that psychoanalysis rested on the correct foundation, but was employing incorrect methods: "With over-determination at any price, one can naturally interpret everything and fit everything in. / One comes necessarily, to the original [Ur-] foundation of things. / And that there are no coincidences is self-evident. / To deny that would be to deny causality. Everything is conditioned, but the problem is finding the correct steps to walk down to the original foundation of things" ("Über Psychoanalyse" 277). Despite Schnitzler's acceptance of the fundamental premise of psychoanalysis, causality, he refused to accept Freud's science as particularly helpful. In a letter to Theodor Reik of December 13, 1913, written in regard to Reik's study, *Arthur Schnitzler als Psycholog,* Schnitzler commended the psychoanalyst on his assessment of conscious elements in the author's work. He insisted, however, that he knew more of his own un- and mid-conscious than Reik. There were more paths leading to the darkness of the soul, Schnitzler wrote, than psychoanalysts dream (*Letters 1913–31* 35).

One must observe the inadequacy of Schnitzler's criticism of Freud's work: his dismissal of the science in the passage from his notes was not in any way conclusive or convincing; after accepting the primacy of causality he did not recommend any methodology for its use in uncovering secrets of the human mind. The critique offered to Reik is a purely personal response. Surely Schnitzler would not suggest that all humans were better than trained professionals in exploring their unconscious minds. Yet in his very personal albeit inconsistent attack on the new science, we can see a prefiguration of Schnitzler's response to the problem of determinism/materialism *in toto.*

The attempt to accurately determine Schnitzler's position vis-à-vis these philosophical issues is complicated. It is insufficient, though tempting and not inaccurate, to posit simply, as Wolfgang Nehring did, that "in later years, Schnitzler's determinism seems to give way to the idea of personal responsibility" (189). But in writing of "Flucht in die Finsternis" Swales commented that there was a polarity throughout Schnitzler's work between to what extent one's actions were pre-determined versus the extent of free will (130). And we have already discussed the similarity of the very early story, "Der Sohn," with the late novel, *Therese,* along these very lines.

Nevertheless it is clear that Schnitzler *wanted* not to be obligated to believe in a deterministic-materialistic world view. Whether from his reading of Helmholtz' essays (Lederer 276), or his attendance at the University of Vienna Medical School, or both, Schnitzler seemed confronted with a *Weltanschauung* demanded by his science, yet unpalatable to him. As the son of a doctor, and himself a physician, Schnitzler "thus stood, from his youth, under the influence of the scientific tradition of the nineteenth century . . . thus is explained the tendency of the young medical student toward materialism and determinism . . . and the attempt to conceive of reality as a great causal connection. Under the influence of scientific thought, Schnitzler developed his skepticism about the superficiality of people and things" (Rey, *Prosa* 14). The question is whether Rey needed to restrict his description to "the young medical student."

Schnitzler wrote the following on his philosophical concerns as a medical student: "I tried, in my own way, to advance the idea of cell theory, unhampered by actual scientific knowledge — I took myself to be a materialist and atheist, and was then exactly as little of either as I am today" (*Jugend in Wien* 94). Yet, as evidenced in his journal entries of 1880, and even in very late works, determinism held an allure for him. At the conclusion of his autobiography Schnitzler simply posited *a priori* the existence of free will. There were individuals, he submitted, "who meet their life-decisions by free choice, even when they think they are being driven by coincidences and moods" (316). This postulation of free will is virtually antithetical to the approaches of both Meynert and Freud.

In his aphorisms, which the author intended to serve as his true opinions on various issues (7), Schnitzler finally struck a balance between free will and determinism. Here he echoed his view of free will as God's agent in man's mind (Lederer 277). He wrote that determinism without free will was fatalism, while the reverse case was arrogance (241).

This conclusion followed an argument in which Schnitzler seemed to have abandoned the scientific perspective. He recognized that for the consistent determinist, belief in free will was in absolute contradiction to the scientific point of view. But, he continued, that perception was itself only of a scientific nature. There were other types of perceptions, as, for example, presentiments (*Ahnungen*). Not that the presentiments, as such, were reality, but rather the necessity, the desire, the compulsion to surmise was real (*Aphorismen* 241). Schnitzler's entry is reminiscent of arguments insisting upon the validity of religion, as presented by Freud in *The Future of an Illusion* (39–40). The psychoanalyst's reply to Schnitzler probably could be taken from the same source: "there is no appeal to a court above that of reason" (43).

Hartmut Scheible, in *Literarischer Jugendstil in Wien* (1984), raised an interesting connection. He noted that the aesthete and positivist were bound by an extreme subjectivism: for the aesthete, nothing outside his own subject was actual, while for the positivist, there was no certainty beyond that of subjective sensate experience (160). Nevertheless, as Scheible had noted earlier, all of the authors associated with aestheticism in Schnitzler's Vienna moved outside its confines: *l'art pour l'art* proved insufficient for all of them. Schnitzler was no pure aesthete, nor was he a total positivist or materialist either. He departed from all these in the process of allowing for supernatural phenomena.

Schnitzler was very blunt about his attitude in an interview with George Sylvester Viereck in 1930. "I am turning away more and more," he said, "from my earlier mechanistic conceptions. I believe in Free Will. Man is responsible for his actions. I could not live in a world without responsibility . . ." (Nehring 189). But Nehring was wrong, as noted above, to interpret Schnitzler's works according to the wishes of the author. He commented that this citation from Viereck, "finds expression in many of the later works . . ." (189).

In the matter of determinism and free will Schnitzler adopted the essential position of the Helmholtz School, as represented by the modified view of Brücke. The physiologist was no atheist and was willing to allow exceptions to an absolute materialist interpretation of events. So, too, Schnitzler rejected for pragmatic rather than logical grounds a purely material world. Free will was a necessary weapon against absurdity. Yet, "if you ask me to prove that the will is free," the author admitted to Viereck, "I must confess my inability" (Worbs 198, n. 33). Our whole existence rests upon three problematical suppositions, Schnitzler wrote near the end of his *Aphorismen.* First, we suppose humanity to be the midpoint of the world. Second, we assume our self represents the midpoint of humanity, and finally, that within our self, there operates an effective free will. Schnitzler continued, "yet, as dubious as all these assumptions might appear, we must accept them as well established and proven, as otherwise our work, our striving, our laws, our hate, our love, our conscience, yes, indeed, our selves would have to be abandoned" (343).

As we have seen, Schnitzler had great difficulty, and expended much effort wrestling with the problem of free will. Neuburger's comment about Rokitansky applies equally well to Schnitzler. Both men were far from contending "that the mechanistic method of research, which . . . conformed to human cognitive capacities, was capable of completely solving the problems of life" ("Rokitansky als Vorkämpfer" 4–5). Schnitzler's late works do not display, with the exception of "Traumnovelle," a movement away from determinism, but only a more sophisticated understanding and portrayal of that perspective. Consequently, one must dispute Scheible's point that in his birthday letter to

Schnitzler, Freud "in the order of qualities that bound him with Schnitzler, [placed] 'determinism' in the first position, not without cause" (*Aufklärung* 49–50). Rather, it was the second broad characteristic mentioned by Freud, skepticism, from which Schnitzler never strayed.

In his *Aphorismen* Schnitzler differentiated between two types of skepticism: the first was a doubting at any price, while the other was the acceptance of an argument only after examination and testing. The second form was, to Schnitzler, the fulfillment of a human duty, while the first was simply a "negative gullibility" (22–23). Schnitzler was himself a practitioner of the second type. He wrote: "That which I call my belief is only the expression for the most plausible explanation of a certain phenomenon, based upon my predisposition, experience, and mode of thought" (*Aphorismen* 18). Throughout his life Schnitzler refused to accept any body of thought *in toto*. "He abhorred dogma of any kind, whether psychological, religious, or patriotic" (Lawson 71).

We have seen that Schnitzler disliked the often unnecessary and excessive probing of the human unconscious advocated, in his view, by psychoanalysis. But the real basis of his criticism of Freud's science was the systematization or generalization of psychological observations which it represented. In fact, Schnitzler wrote, "precisely by generalizing its theories, for example the Oedipus complex, psychoanalysis reduces their significance. If it is really the fate of every person to love his mother and hate his father, then this circumstance is a phenomenon of evolution, like all others . . . and becomes uninteresting" ("Über Psychoanalyse" 278). And again, a bit later, he asks, what is won and what squandered in making psychoanalysis into a system, thereby allowing it to become modish? (280).

Actually, Schnitzler denied the possibility of systematically obtaining an accurate overview of the total human personality. A real understanding of humankind, in the true sense of the word, was always a matter of intuition (*Der Geist im Wort* 22). This sentiment is almost antithetical to Freud's position in *Future of an Illusion:* "scientific work is the only road which can lead us to a knowledge of reality outside ourselves. It is once again merely an illusion to expect anything from intuition . . . ," except particulars of one's own mental life (50). Robert O. Weiss interpreted Schnitzler's rejection of psychoanalysis as part of a tendency to question many conceptions to which he was exposed, beginning in his medical education ("A Study of Psychiatric Elements" 252).

Schnitzler's repudiation of organized religion was as vehement as Freud's, but only in his unpublished, youthful writings. In these, the budding dramatist was biting in his criticism of religion, and especially of Christianity. Diary entries for 1880, the beginning of the period in which Schnitzler most concerned himself with religious questions (*Jugend in Wien* 94), are particularly venomous and supercilious. For example, the eighteen-year-old wrote of the uneducated always requiring a religion, and the unhappy uneducated more urgently than others (*Tagebuch* 4/29/80). And on March 19 of the same year Schnitzler filled almost three pages with invective against Christianity. The Evangelists had perverted the religion totally, while Jesus himself had been merely a great actor, too clever himself to believe in a God. He allowed himself to be crucified, however, to give the world a belief in God.

The topic of religion in general appears to have lost much of its fascination for Schnitzler. In his literary works religion was never a major theme. Like Freud, Schnitzler recognized the potentiality of religious belief. Indeed, in his last work, *Therese,* the possible consolation of religion was affirmed. When she learns of her mother's death and is turned away from her brother's house, Therese, after a long absence, once again enters a church: "And again it occurred, as so often in past years, that in the half-darkness of the lofty, incense-scented room, a wonderful peace came over her, an other and deeper peace than that of the stillness of a wood or a mountain meadow, or any other solitude by which she had felt blessed" (211). The narrator attributes a special quality to Therese's church attendance, something that transcends, say, an experience in nature. It was the trappings of religion that the mature Schnitzler deprecated, not, like Freud, religious belief itself.

Similarly Schnitzler did not disdain spritualism. Though he considered the belief in miracles to be psycho-pathological, he wrote to Danish critic Georg Brandes that such beliefs were to be found in the healthiest brain as well (3/13/1906). And in a late letter to Dr. Auernheimer (5/14/28) Schnitzler pointed to his *Aphorismen* as evidence that he did not deny the existence of a supernatural world (Just 107). Further, in a wartime diary entry, Schnitzler recorded that he was awakened from a shallow sleep, as though by a pistol shot. He told his wife that they should note the hour, for perhaps an acquaintance had just then fallen in battle (*Tagebuch* 1/10/15).

Clearly, however, the thrust of Schnitzler's aphorisms was toward the rational rather than the mystical. For example, in considering the transmigration of souls, the author insisted on compelling his reader to attempt to visualize such a process. Schnitzler concluded that those who believed in this phenomenon had not really thought the matter through. Rather, he saw belief in transmigration as another bit of folly in which humans indulged to make existence less mundane (*Aphorismen* 179). And though in an observation of 1904 Schnitzler postulated cellular recollection, à la Freud, but with the intent of thereby evidencing a relation between the present and a past existence, he later (1924) insisted that everything in our unconscious had to have come through our consciousness: "inherited things in the unconscious," he states flatly, "do not exist" ("Über Psychologie" 277, 281).

When he approached the subject of religion at all, Schnitzler, like Freud, did so from the outside, that is, more for its sociological interest than for its emotional or psychological effects. The type of sentiment apparent in the passage from *Therese* was infrequent in Schnitzler's oeuvre. To a greater extent than Freud, who, after all, had dealt with religion generally, for example, in *The Future of an Illusion*, Schnitzler confined himself to considering Judaism, indeed, more specifically, to the social issue of the "Jewish Question." In his treatment Schnitzler was unrivaled. Frederick J. Beharriell judged correctly when he submitted that "no author has written more authoritatively, more frankly, and yet with such utter impartiality of the Jewish problem as has Schnitzler in *Professor Bernhardi, Der Weg ins Freie . . .*" (Beharriell, "Range" 307), and, it might be added, in his autobiography. There are no very thorough references to Judaism or anti-Semitism in Schnitzler's journals. After his student years, the dramatist did not give vent to religious thoughts, if he entertained any. There are not infrequent complaints about the treatment allotted to Jews, as on February 11, 1898, when Schnitzler confessed that he had been aggravated by the infamous attacks to which one, as a Jew, was exposed. Yet, Schnitzler turned a cold shoulder to esoteric Judaism as well. After visiting fellow author Richard Beer-Hofmann, he complained of that writer's specialized relation to Judaism and of his interest which seemed confined to Zionist problems (*Tagebuch* 1/13/22).

A somewhat more developed picture of the "Jewish Question," and a more detailed account of anti-Semitism in fin-de-siècle Vienna is provided in Schnitzler's *Jugend in Wien*. The author's impartiality or clinical objectivity is well-exemplified in his treatment of Mayor Karl Lueger, who won office on an anti-Semitic platform. Even at the height of his popularity, Schnitzler noted, Lueger was as little an anti-Semite as when he had played the Austrian card game, Tarock, with his Jewish friends at the home of Dr. Ferdinand Mandl. Schnitzler continued: "There were, and there are people who counted it a good quality in him that, even in his strongest period of anti-Semitism, he maintained a certain predilection for many Jews, and made no secret of it. For me it was precisely this that acted as the strongest proof of his moral questionability" (142). Schnitzler, writing late in the First World War, considered consistent prejudice to be more virtuous than random intolerance. He did not realize to what an extent his sentiments approached those of Adolf Hitler, who wrote, less than a year after the War, that anti-Semitism "on purely emotional grounds will find its ultimate expression in the form of pogroms. The anti-Semitism of reason . . . however, must lead to a systematic and legal struggle against, and eradication of, what privileges the Jews now enjoy . . ." (Rubenstein, "The Unmastered Trauma" 160). One doubts that Schnitzler would have found Hitler's consistency to be a sign of his probity, nor can one imagine the author, despite his medical education, retaining the objectivity he displayed here.

It is clear that Schnitzler was deeply offended by anti-Semitism throughout the period documented in his autobiography (1862–1889). He cited the infamous Waidhofener Resolution at length, even though the anti-Semitic prohibition against fighting duels with Jews came seven years outside the purview of *Jugend in Wien* (3/11/96). He commented that Jews had from necessity become such excellent duelists that the German nationalists had to protect themselves as best they could (*Jugend* 152).

In his autobiography Schnitzler also described the case of a friend, Louis Friedmann, which must have led the author to a profounder understanding of the "Jewish Question." Louis, of Jewish heritage, was determined to remain single, or at least childless, so as not to transmit to further generations the hated Jewish blood running through his veins. Schnitzler obtained a certain satisfaction when overhearing a group of Friedmann's hiking companions. They all conceded Louis' ability, but one of the group admitted that he nevertheless felt an aversion to Friedmann, as he did to all Jews (205). Schnitzler's satisfaction rested, apparently, on his evaluation of Friedmann's attitude as dishonest, or in some other way reprehensible.

His description of Louis' case is an example of Schnitzler's approach to anti-Semitism. He was fascinated, he wrote, not by the political or social aspects of the Jewish Question, but predominantly by the psychological side. His objectivity came easily to him, despite the occasional anger expressed in private, for he was, he believed, totally unmoved by the "confessional impulse" (*Jugend* 93). In his depiction of Louis Friedmann, as in fictional portrayals of the *Judenfrage*, Schnitzler was content with mere description: unlike Freud, no etiology was attempted, but like Freud, and in the tradition of therapeutic skepticism, no judgment was made; no solution offered or even sought.

Although *Professor Bernhardi* presents various shadings of the "Jewish Question" quite well, Schnitzler seems to have virtually poured his ideas concerning this issue into the novel he wrote partially at the same time as *Bernhardi, Der Weg ins Freie*. Schnitzler was in a small group in thinking his novel a great work of art, and his self-admiration reached alarming proportions late in his life. In 1929, following a reading of the work for a proposed film version, the author found it extraordinary and virtually in a class of its own (*Tagebuch* 4/13/29). Yet, the poet to whom the work was dedicated, Hugo von Hofmannsthal, left it lying "half accidentally, half intentionally, in a train" (A.S., *Briefe 1875–1912* 631); and, early in 1908, Schnitzler had to battle his publisher, Samuel Fischer's, suggestion that the first chapter be omitted altogether for its lack of interest (A.S., *Briefe 1875–1912* 566–576).

Schnitzler insisted in a letter to Leonie Meyerhof-Hildeck (7/12/1908) that one might excise all reference to the Jewish Question and *Der Weg* would remain a fairly comprehensive book (*Briefe 1875–1912* 583). Nevertheless, the novel contains the most extensive expression of its author's ideas regarding the Jewish character, assimilation, Zionism, and anti-Semitism. Schnitzler agreed with Georg Brandes' notion that *Der Weg* was two novels in one: beyond recounting the interaction of the lives of a group of talented and largely Jewish Viennese, the novel was the love story of composer Georg von Wergenthin and Anna Rosner. The reader finds little relationship between the two strands of the work which Schnitzler held to be equally important to him. He continued his letter to Brandes (7/4/1908) by explaining that in *Der Weg* "I have in fact reflected a year in the life of Baron von Wergenthin, in which he comes to an understanding of all sorts of people and problems, and of himself" (*Briefe 1875–1912* 579). Schnitzler's simplistic explanation of the novel's focus does not go far toward explaining why the vast majority of the gentile composer's friends are Jewish.

The fact that Georg is a gentile allows the narrator to filter Jewish actions and arguments through a more typically European consciousness. The reader of *Der Weg* is offered the means to observe the dynamics of anti-Semitism, which is not the case in much scholarly work concerning the Holocaust. The latter, according to Rubenstein, has tended to "emphasize what was done to the Jews rather than those elements of conflict and competition between Jews and non-Jews . . ." (Rubenstein, "Unmastered Trauma" 129). What Schnitzler's quite objective portrayal of Jewish-gentile interaction reveals is a problem for which neither the protagonist, nor, one imagines, his creator, had the solution. It is clear, as Andrew Török noted, that Schnitzler's own opinions were most nearly those of the Jewish writer, Heinrich Bermann, and that Bermann is the hero of the work in that he is confronted by all problems: as a lover, a Jew, and an artist (373–374). Georg's relations to Heinrich are, in fact, representative of his response to Jews more generally. After an early meeting, "Georg watched [Heinrich] with interest (or 'sympathy': *Teilnahme*) and repugnance together" (*Weg* 52), and following their last conversation, Georg "knew that this person was not to be helped" (330).

Georg's attitude towards the Jews who surround him is ambivalent. He shows himself to be a sensitive observer, as when he detects a tendency toward shame among Jews, indeed, the inevitability of either shame or fear. "He only encountered Jews," we read, "who were ashamed to be Jews, or those who were proud, and feared that one would believe they were ashamed" (33). The tremendous defensiveness or hypersensitivity eventually and occasionally annoys Georg. When Heinrich describes his father as a tragicomic figure, being, as he was, a Jewish patriot, Georg replies that Heinrich seems monomaniacal: "one really gets the impression sometimes that you are altogether no longer capable of seeing anything in the world besides the Jewish Question, always and everywhere." The composer then introduces the possibility of a persecution mania which Heinrich, in the very ferocity of his denial, appears in fact to approach. What Georg chooses to call a persecution mania, Heinrich counters, is in truth nothing other than "an uninterrupted, alert, very intensive knowledge of a condition in which we Jews find ourselves. Rather than persecution mania, one could speak of a mania for safety, of a mania for being left in peace . . ." (203).

Schnitzler had gently, perhaps unintentionally touched upon links among insanity, creativity and Jewishness in his story "Mein Freund Ypsilon." There, the fine and delicate line that separates insanity from creativity was established. It was noted that the letter "Y" was often used to signify a Jew (Bakan 38), though there are no other references to "Y"'s religion in the tale. However, in *Der Weg ins Freie,* Schnitzler cited a number of cases of insanity among the Jews. Bermann's father had gone mad, and following the conversation just cited, Georg thinks that Heinrich "was, in his own way, just as sick as his father. Yet, one could not say that he had had any bad experiences personally." Without realizing it, Georg's reflections, as they develop, hit upon the likely cause of the frequency of Jewish insanity. Heinrich, the composer observes, "had once maintained that he felt no sense of belonging with anyone. That is not true. He has a sense of belonging with all Jews, and feels closer to the last of these than to me" (205). One imagines this a not unusual belief among gentiles. Yet, earlier, Heinrich had told Georg the story of a Polish Jew traveling in a train compartment with a stranger. The Jew behaves perfectly until he becomes aware that his companion is also a Jew, "whereupon he immediately stretched his legs onto the seat across from him, and sighed a relieved 'ä soi.'" Heinrich interprets this as a very "profound" insight into the "tragicomedy" of contemporary Judaism, and likens the situation of modern Jews to that of prisoners in an enemy's country (127–128). This lack of respect for Jewish coreligionists because of a shared religion or race can accentuate an isolation wrought by living in an alien culture.

In fact, after Georg quips that Heinrich seems more anti-Semitic than most Christians he knows, the writer does not disagree. He relates that Jews are reared to be particularly sensitive to Jewish characteristics and foibles. When a Jew is rude or ridiculous in his presence, Heinrich confesses, such a strong feeling of embarrassment befalls him that he vainly wishes to sink into the ground. He feels shame for these Jews, but his hatred is reserved for those who attempt to conceal their heritage (128). Despite understanding that concealment might offer relief from the pressures of being a Jew, Heinrich rejects this dishonesty, as he does conversion (96). Jews in modern European society are depicted in Schnitzler's novel as being under great stress. Heinrich's father, the patriot-Jew, goes insane. Another Jew, whose father had publicly humiliated him for paying obeisance to Catholics leaving Church, attempts suicide (194). Leo Golowski, who suffers from the anti-Semitism of his commander, First Lieutenant Sefranek, kills the man in a duel and goes to jail. His sister's boyfriend insists that Sefranek was "as little an anti-Semite as . . . I." Rather, Leo is at fault; he "suffers decidedly from a sickly sensitivity." And when her friend generalizes his opinion to include all Jews ("it's really as though these people were insane"), Leo's sister responds, simply, "he could be right there" (189, 190). Whether due to forces from without, within, or both, the Jew, in Schnitzler's depiction, was in an uncomfortable or perhaps untenable position in modern Europe. The second possibility formed the basis for the central argument concerning the Jewish Question: was Zionism the best alternative? As Georg listens, Leo Golowski argues in favor of a Jewish fatherland, while Bermann represents the opposing view.

Despite the realization that his father, as a Jewish patriot, was a tragicomic figure, Heinrich insists that Jews must assimilate, they must strive to be more than merely tolerated. Leo finds that hope an impossibility. He posits an underlying difference between Jews and others, one which makes coexistence unbearable. Heinrich, Leo feels, is not even aware of the magnitude of the differences separating the groups involved. Leo is not thinking of commonplace, omnipresent anti-Semitism. "In the first place," he says, "this does not deal with you . . . and also not with the few Jewish officials who do not advance, the few Jewish volunteers who do not become officers, the Jewish university lecturers who do not receive professorships, or are granted them belatedly" (92). These are annoyances of a second degree of importance. But at the Zionist Congress at Basel Leo had met people who, not merely resentful of discrimination, wanted to found a homeland, from a "yearning for Palestine." So great was this desire that old men had wept when a speaker alluded to the dim chances for Palestinian settlement (92–93). Heinrich argues that the idea of a Fatherland is fictitious, "a political concept, pending [and] variable." What is real, he asserts, is only the homeland, the feeling and rights (or "laws": *Recht*) of the homeland (93). Zionism might be valid as a moral principle or as an action for the welfare of the people, but the establishment of a Jewish state upon religious and nationalistic foundations appeared to him as against the grain of the spirit of historical development (93).

Georg acts as the objective observer: he senses the value of both arguments. His sympathy shifts from Leo, who with a glowing compassion wants to spare his compatriots from people who spurn them as different, to Heinrich, who sees the Zionist enterprise as threatening to lure Jews who had made and attained great heights in other nation's cultures to a land for which they felt no homesickness whatever. For the first time, Georg comes to understand the problem and the fate of the European Jew; the desire to feel at home and to work for one's country, coupled with the fear of being seen as an intruder if one rose too high or even strove too hard (94). And Georg observes at the same time that the silhouette of Heinrich, who was arguing for assimilation, resembled a fanatical Jewish preacher, while the Zionist Leo was reminiscent of a Greek youth. Schnitzler wanted to guarantee against typecasting.

In fact Heinrich is not nearly so convinced of his assimilationist argument as he would have his listeners believe. He is far too aware of the cleavage between races. When talking with Georg, in a later scene, the author argues that Jews, from necessity, understand Christians far better than vice versa. "This task of understanding," he explains, had to develop in us in the course of time . . . following the laws of the battle for existence, if you will" (129). That was part of the price of accommodating to an enemy's environment (*Feindesland*). When Georg protests that he is now arguing contrarily to his position vis-à-vis Leo, Heinrich responds:

"the matter is much too complicated to ever be settled. Even internally it is nearly impossible. And now, moreover, in words! Yes, sometimes one would like to believe that things were not so bad. Sometimes, one is really at home, despite everything, one feels so at home here... " (129). Heinrich does not know the answer to the Jewish Question, nor did Schnitzler, Andrew Török noted that Schnitzler came no closer to reconciling the various parts of this problem than he did in solving the problems wrought by love within the novel (376).

There is yet another revealing, though much less important discussion of Zionism, between Herr Ehrenberg, the father who shamed his son, and Edmund Nürnberger. The latter is an inactive writer who fits Schnitzler's first definition of a skeptic: one who doubts at any price. Ehrenberg, a wealthy merchant, expresses the desire to see Jerusalem before dying. He has read much about Zionism, and comments that perhaps it is "the only way out." When Nürnberger observes that anti-Semitism does not seem to have affected Ehrenberg's standard of living, the merchant contends that he would gladly part with half his fortune to see the worst of the Jews' foes strung up. And when Nürnberger counters that he would worry that the incorrect ones might be hanged, Ehrenberg rejoins, "the danger is not great . . . grab the one next door, and you'll catch one" (60).

The scene develops further along the lines suggested here. Ehrenberg is presented as another somewhat paranoid Jew, while Nürnberger finds it necessary to remain aloof and cool. He is not baptized, but remarks that he is in any case no longer a Jew either, "for the simple reason that I never felt like a Jew." Ehrenberg, in anger, cannot accept that posture: "if one punched in your top hat . . . because you have a somewhat Jewish nose, you would feel yourself struck as a Jew . . ." (61).

Nürnberger is an example of a type of Jew that Georg describes late in the novel: "too-smart, pitiless, a keen understander of his fellow man . . . the main thing for him remains that he not let himself be surprised by anything" (216). Nürnberger predicts the end of Georg's love for Anna, and his prediction proves to be correct. By assuming the worst of human beings, Heinrich says of the cynic, "he always maintains the right. One can never be betrayed if one mistrusts everything on earth, even one's own mistrust . . ." (326). Yet Nürnberger is unable to produce, or create. Again Bermann supplies the reason: fruitfulness is apportioned to wrath, but not to disgust (198). Nürnberger's aloofness and mistrust spare him pain, whether as a Jew or more generally as a human, but he is unable to feel and unable to write.

None of the Jewish types depicted in *Der Weg ins Freie* offers an answer to the Jewish question. Frederick Beharriell, in arguing that Schnitzler's range of theme was broader than the commonly conceded subjects of love and death, wrote that the author dealt with "many things, but only as those things clarify, symbolize, or in some way lay bare the functioning of personality. In his studies of . . . the Jewish problem . . . we find no answers to the age-old questions . . . what we do find are shrewd revelations of the infinite complexity of the human mind and heart" (310). Norbert Abel observed that both Schnitzler and Freud lacked a theory with which to approach anti-Semitism. This conclusion applies to the playwright more accurately than to the psychoanalyst. Despite the not-so-quiet desperation of both men in the face of this prejudice, Freud has been able to explain anti-Semitism within psychoanalytical thought. For Schnitzler, as we have seen, the psychological dimension of the entire Jewish Question was paramount. How did a gentile respond to the Jews; how did the Jew live with his Jewishness in an anti-Semitic society; what were the real strengths and weaknesses in Zionism and assimilationism: these were the questions that interested Schnitzler. The author did not seek the etiology of anti-Semitism, as had Freud, and certainly did not have a solution to offer.

One must take into account that Schnitzler died in 1931. He was well aware of anti-Semitic developments in Germany and Austria and experienced some annoyance at the hands of Nazi *provocateurs* (*Tagebuch* 11/3/22). But as his assessment of Karl Lueger suggested, the author could not foresee even the outlines of Hitler's Final Solution. There is a gruesome irony in *Der Weg*.

Following their debate concerning Zionism, Leo asks Heinrich what he would do if the funeral pyres of the Inquisition were rekindled. Bermann admits that he would then become a Zionist. Georg, who has been listening, submits that "those times will certainly not come again." The others laugh, "that Georg, with these words, was so kind as to reassure them about their future, in the name of entire Christendom" (96). Schnitzler could not have imagined the grisly twist which retrospection would give this conversation, written thirty years before the Anschluss.

Willehad Eckert interpreted Schnitzler as an obstinate Jew (*Trotzjude* 119), into which category Freud, too, might fit. Schnitzler, had he lived, might well have insisted upon his Jewishness, as Freud did, particularly under adverse circumstances. Yet in the relatively halcyon teens and twenties Schnitzler stressed that he was a German author (Eckert 123), and rejected Zionism in both his autobiography and *Der Weg ins Freie* (Eckert 122). But like Heinrich Bermann in the novel Schnitzler was most unrelenting in his opposition to conversion, to what he interpreted as excessive attempts to fit in (Eckert 125). For the author, conversion was a dishonest attempt to be something one was not.

In his examination of the Jewish Question, as elsewhere, one perceives that Schnitzler's skepticism was a constant: that spirit of objective inquiry which the therapeutic skeptics had reintroduced into medicine remained in full force with Schnitzler, while his determinism wavered. Henri Ellenberger was only a little more than half correct in concluding that Schnitzler in *Der Geist im Wort und der Geist in der Tat* and his *Aphorismen* "revealed himself as much less skeptical than one would have thought from his earlier literary work. He took a stand against the theory of universal determinism . . . his belief in the existence of God is expressed, though in veiled terms" (473).

One can agree with Ellenberger's conclusion, particularly concerning Schnitzler's stance toward determinism, though, as we have seen, his rejection of both materialism and determinism were more a matter of desire than a result of reasoning. The second half of Ellenberger's contention is more problematic. For Schnitzler,

"God" seems to have been a synonym for first cause, as was revealed in the discussion concerning free will versus determinism.
One of Schnitzler's aphorisms lends itself particularly well to an
interpretation of the author's theism, especially if it is gleaned
superficially: "whatever you believe: be it in the existence of a
highest being, providence, conscience, will, fate, divine justice, or
none of these, but rather in the total absurdity of the world and of
existence: you have only meant God" (175). Schnitzler was
addressing the concept of belief in this aphorism, more so than
theism. Accepting one possibility on faith involved the same
suspension of critical perspective as did accepting another. Belief
in any of the possibilities listed by Schnitzler signified an identical
abandonment of responsibility: like illness and insanity, belief
could be employed as excuse. In another aphorism Schnitzler had
noted that it was a person of a higher type for whom freedom
represented something other than the desire for irresponsibility
(Swales 42). In the event it seems highly improbable that Schnitzler believed in the God that Freud defined as common: an authori-
tarian father-figure.

As we have seen, in his public posture Freud seemed content
to rely on the scientific *Weltanschauung*. This signified little more
than the willingness to rely on science to answer the problems of
existence, and the belief that science could best do so. Schnitzler
was even skeptical of this belief. He would not accept any world
view as the term was defined by Freud. Wolfgang Nehring wrote
that once Schnitzler "defended himself against the reproach that
he had no deeper *Weltanschauung* . . . with the answer that for
him 'world-contemplation' (*Weltbetrachtung*) . . . was enough"
(189).

CONCLUSION

"What People Call Pessimism"

Freud's perception of his affinity with Schnitzler was based upon their shared determinism, skepticism, and ultimately, pessimism (page 1, above). These three elements of a *Weltanschauung* were fundamental aspects of the intellectual climate at the University of Vienna Medical School, which both men attended. Two major debates: concerning the possibility or even desirability of helping the ill, and the validity of the materialist world-view, offer an inroad into the mature thought and work of both men. These controversies, in which both Schnitzler and Freud were indirectly involved, through their instructors, provide a useful context in attempting to explain specific attitudes not only toward science and medicine, but also toward the treatment of fundamental themes in the works of both. Yet though the thesis of this study is that both authors' views of life were profoundly affected by their medical school training, the very titles of Chapters Two and Three reflect that they responded differently to the faculty's projected influence.

Especially in the case of Freud, one must draw a distinction between the public and private man. As we have seen in Chapter Two, Freud as a scientist depicted himself as a skeptic, an unbeliever. That any conclusion must be based upon examined evidence was the foundation of the Second Viennese Medical School, and was part of Freud's definition of the scientific *Weltanschauung* (*New Introductory Lectures* 159). Freud's insistence upon remaining a nominal Jew, after revealing the origins of religion to be infantile wish-fulfillment, his excessive cigar-smoking, and his dabbling in mental telepathy were all decisions not empirically founded. Freud dealt with this seeming inconsistency by relegating his illogical stances to the private sphere which was no one else's concern. Nevertheless Freud's skepticism or scientific objectivity also lapsed in his "public" acceptance of Lamarck's theory of the inheritance of acquired characteristics, even though he was aware that Lamarck had been refuted (Jones 3, 335). The utilization of an outdated biological theory by Freud reflected the depth of the psychoanalyst's determinism. All human action was determined by motives, and the business of science, of psychoanalysis, was to reveal those motives. Psychoanalysis had shown that the very foundation of civilization and religion was the attempt to deal with the feeling of guilt which must have been transmitted genetically, according to Freud. Thus Lamarck, right or wrong, fitted into the psychoanalytic interpretation. One may say, then, that Freud's skepticism gave way before his determinism.

Quite the opposite was true of Schnitzler. Though the author's only registered response to Freud's letter of May 14, 1922 was that it was lovely (schön) (Tagebuch 5/19/22), the discussion in Chapter Three demonstrates the dissimilarity of the two men concerning the role of determinism and skepticism in their world-view. While Freud's devotion to psychoanalysis grew, and his determinism consequently firmed, Schnitzler's skepticism vanquished all systems, including Freud's science and determinism. Yet the poet's transcendence of determinism, his postulation of free will, was not based on logical reasoning, but rather on pragmatic arguments and personal necessity.

The varying perspective of these two graduates of the University of Vienna Medical School is epitomized by their respective comments concerning war. For Freud, as one might expect, war represented confirmation that "aggressive instincts were stronger than contemporary civilized man had believed" (Ellenberger 473). European civilization, Freud wrote in his essay, "Reflections upon War and Death" (1915), was itself an illusion, and "we must not then complain if now and again [illusions] come into conflict with some portion of reality, and are shattered against it" (Rieff, *Freud: Character and Culture* 113). Freud's reasoning followed the lines established in *Totem and Taboo* and *Civilization and Its Discontents* concerning man's fundamentally aggressive nature. He noted that "the very emphasis of the commandment *Thou shalt not kill* makes it certain that we spring from an endless ancestry of murderers" (Rieff, *Character* 129). The ostensible causes of war, such as economic conflicts, were merely rationalizations of emotions: nations "parade their interests as their justification for satisfying their passions" (Rieff, *Character* 121). The psychoanalyst concluded his essay of 1915 with the dire prediction that war would continue. "War is not to be abolished," Freud concluded, "so long as the conditions of existence among the nations are so varied, and the repulsion between peoples so intense, there *will be, must be* wars" (Rieff, *Character* 133, my emphasis).

Freud considered war again in an open letter to Albert Einstein, entitled "Why War," written in September 1932. Though his view of war's cause had not changed, the tone of the letter was more optimistic than its predecessor of 1915. Freud suggested that wars might be prevented by the establishment of a "central authority to which the right of giving judgment upon all conflicts of interest shall be handed over" (Rieff, *Character* 139). The best possible situation was, ultimately, a "dictatorship of reason," a world in which man had subordinated instinctual life to what Freud had called in *The Future of an Illusion*, the soft voice of the intellect (Rieff, *Character* 145).

Arthur Schnitzler had kept a notebook of observations about war which was published under the title *Über Krieg und Frieden* in 1939. His position, as expressed in these notes, was antithetical to Freud's concerning the fundamental convictions here under consideration. War, the playwright submitted, was neither a historical necessity nor an expression of true human nature: "dogma says: war is necessitated by fate; it is founded upon the organization of human nature. This dogma is false. War is not founded upon human nature, but in the substance of state-formation, and in the relations of individual states" (*Über Krieg* 21). An individual might well desire action, danger, or adventure, but never war (44). Man was, more or less, duped into conceiving of war as relating to larger ideas, and was therefore willing to die for, say, a piece of land that actually meant nothing to him (30). Just as Schnitzler saw the etiology of war quite differently than Freud, his solution was also of another order. In discussing peace, the poet wrote, as though with Freud in mind, one must exclude all notions of the possibility that humans would become better or smarter in the foreseeable future (31). Freud's belief in the efficacy of an international organization and a society based upon reason was, for Schnitzler, pure fantasy. The only path to peace was to rearrange relations in the world so that not a single person could profit from war. If the elimination of gain through war were impossible, Schnitzler concluded, then so too was peace (29).

The differences in these two views of war highlight the conclusions reached in Chapters Two and Three. For Freud, war was the natural eruption of human destructive impulses. Near the beginning of World War One (11/25/14), he wrote Lou Andreas-Salomé that "the saddest thing of all is that [the War] is precisely what psychoanalysis had led us to expect of man and his behavior" (Schur 91–92). Yet at least human reason might someday bring an end to man's aggressive behavior by subjugating the impulses.

Schnitzler rejected a deterministic interpretation of war: he saw such conflicts as expressions of commercial or economic competition. But his perspective was far more skeptical in regard to the human capacity for change or improvement. In making war, according to the poet, man was not following an unconscious urge, was not at the mercy of his impulses, but on the darker side Schnitzler implied the unlikelihood that conditions would improve. The great mistake was to base plans or hopes for future peace upon any improvement of human behavior.

Rather than being inherently aggressive, Schnitzler saw man as innately apathetic. In his notes on war, the author included the observation that "this apathy probably developed in the struggle for existence, for only through it was life, and the continuation of life, made possible . . . In reality, we are all without compassion. Our heart sees exactly ten paces ahead" (*Über Krieg* 40). Like Freud, who had argued that we could not share another's suffering (*Civilization* 36), Schnitzler denied the possibility of compassion, by arguing that apathy was required for survival. "Those who suffer-with ['the compassionate': *Mitleidigen*], in the true sense of the word, must die out" (40).

Compassion was the great hope of Karl von Rokitansky and Theodor Meynert. For these philosophic idealists, it represented the only possibility of breaking free from an egoism imposed by the existence of an incomprehensible noumena. By "suffering with," in their view, one might hope to transcend one's own suffering. For both Freud and Schnitzler, even this small hope did not exist. "What had happened to the [nineteenth] century?" Ludwig Marcuse asked in a similar context. His answer: "it knew too much" (28).

Schnitzler had discarded the possibility of true compassion as early as 1880. He argued in a journal entry of April 29 that egoism and compassion worked against each other, and from all appearances, the former was the dominant principle in the world: each looked out for himself at the expense of the other. Nor was altruism likely to be successful. Schnitzler reasoned that as we were unable to fulfill our own egoistic ends, we were even less likely to succeed in truly improving the lot of others. There can be few better examples than this of William M. Johnston's contention that therapeutic nihilism was a major trend in Viennese thought long after it had departed the faculty of the medical school (71). In rejecting the possibility of compassion, one might add that Schnitzler was even skeptical of the skeptics' one hope.

Schnitzler's doubts concerning man's inclination and ability to help others remained constant from his early medical school days to his death. Freud entertained similar qualms, not only in his general statements in *Civilization* but also, as we have seen, concerning psychoanalysis as a therapeutic tool. Though the prospect of being unable to penetrate the essence of an other is not cheering, a realization of the fact or a postulation of the theory is not of itself pessimistic. Freud overestimated Schnitzler's determinism and his own skepticism. In his letter of May 13, 1922 Freud concluded that the combination of skepticism and determinism were "what people call[ed] pessimism" (page one, above). But "pessimistic" is an inaccurate description of the Viennese playwright. Freud himself had a very precise idea of what pessimism was, as he showed in another letter, to Andreas-Salomé, dated July 30, 1915: "I cannot be an optimist, and I believe I differ from the pessimists only in so far as wicked, stupid, senseless things don't upset me because I have accepted them from the beginning as part of what the world is composed of" (E. Freud 311).

If Schnitzler qualified as a pessimist at all, it was only in the more limited sense of the word, as it relates to one's temperament. Even then, Schnitzler revealed gloom only in the privacy of his journal. Two events in his later life account, in large measure for the author's despair: his unhappy marriage, and the suicide, at age eighteen, of his daughter, Lili (1929). Journal entries for the years 1920, 1921, and 1929 are full of an embittered hopelessness. Yet it was during the 1920s that Schnitzler also wrote his most optimistic work, "Traumnovelle." Unlike Freud, who possessed a "pessimistic and tragic view of life" (Bettelheim 108), Schnitzler was by nature too much the *bon vivant* to despair for very long. He was fully capable of living and enjoying life in a world peopled by the apathetic.

As an artist Schnitzler felt he could rebel against demoralizing doctrines like determinism. Yet skepticism leaves one constantly open to emotional shock. In discussing the two men's views of civilized society, Michael Worbs captured the essential difference between the determinist, Freud, and the skeptic, Schnitzler: "what was for Freud a necessary system was still, for Schnitzler, a cause for suffering" (256).

Differences observed between Freud and Schnitzler in the levels of their skepticism, determinism, and pessimism derived from their respective relationships to the University of Vienna Medical School. Peter Gay observed that Freud's Vienna "was medical Vienna, and *that* city rarely frequented the hospitable mansions of Vienna's patrons" (*Freud, Jews and other Germans,* 34). As a man of science, even in his nonmedical writings, Freud appears bound to the controversies of the medical faculty that trained him, whether by supporting the vitalism of Hyrtl in positing a death impulse, or by manifesting the materialism of Brücke's laboratory in assigning significance to every slip of the tongue.

As a scientist Freud could not discard determinism simply by fiat, as Schnitzler had done, because it was personally repugnant. At the same time the basic tenets of psychoanalysis were, for Freud, beyond questioning, an immunity not granted to them or any other body of ideas by Schnitzler. Finally, Freud's pessimism was either awakened or enhanced by his contact with the University of Vienna Medical School, especially with Theodor Meynert. There was a strong Schopenhauerian influence upon the psychoanalyst. Little influence can be ascribed to the German philosopher in the case of Schnitzler. Rather typically for a "fundamentally unphilosophical person" (Worbs 256), the author's approach to Schopenhauer was through his letters. In his own letter of July 21, 1895, to girlfriend Marie Reinhard, Schnitzler noted curtly that part of his reading now included the great pessimist's letters, but no other reference is made to Schopenhauer in the letters, the journals, or the autobiography of the playwright.

As was the case with his psychological insights, Schnitzler's pessimism, such as it was, came from personal experience. What Freud observed in the birthday letter of May 14, 1922 had a broad application. "I have formed the impression," Freud wrote, "that you know through intuition—or rather from detailed self-observation—everything that I have discovered by laborious work on other people" (E. Freud 339–340).

The differences in fundamental elements of the *Weltanschauungen* of Freud and Schnitzler are functions of their responses to their medical training, which, ultimately, originated in the constitutional or temperamental differences of the scientist and the artist. Perhaps even before distancing himself from the medical school, Schnitzler became a victim of the *Wert-Vakuum* postulated by Hermann Broch (page 2, above), as evidenced by his rejection of the possibility of compassion in 1880. Though he lacked the essential pessimism of Freud, and abandoned determinism, Schnitzler never managed to find a "satisfying meaning in the self" (Schorske 14). For the skeptic if meaning cannot be found within, it will not be found at all. Freud was always closer to the medical school, even despite himself. Through an amalgamation of intellectual trends present in the school, Freud was able to forge a new mode of interpretation, if not of therapy.

WORKS CONSULTED

I. Bibliographies

Allen, Richard H. *An Annotated Arthur Schnitzler Bibliography 1879-1965.* Chapel Hill: University of North Carolina Press, 1966.

Berlin, Jeffrey B. *An Annotated Arthur Schnitzler Bibliography 1965-1977.* München: Wilhelm Fink, 1978.

Meyer-Palmedo, Ingeborg. *Sigmund Freud Konkordanz und Gesamtbibliographie.* Frankfurt am Main: Fischer, 1975.

II. Primary Sources

A. Unpublished

"Hyrtl." TS at the Institut für Geschichte der Medizin, University of Vienna, Abschrift 1111.

"Professor Hyrtl's Rektorsrede." TS at the Institut für Geschichte der Medizin, University of Vienna, Abschrift 72. Rpt. of a feuilleton in *Wiener medizinische Wochenschrift,* October 8, 1864 (14. Jg., Nr. 41).

Rokitansky, Karl von. *Lebenserinnerungen.* TS, dated 1876–1877, at the Institut für Geschichte der Medizin, University of Vienna.

Schnitzler, Arthur. *Tagebücher 1879–1931.* TS at the Archiv der Akademie der Wissenschaften, Kommission für literarische Gebrauchsformen, Werner Welzig, Obmann, Vienna.

B. Published

Anton, G. "Über psychologische Leitgedanken Theodor Meynert's." *Münchener medizinische Wochenschrift*, Separatabdruck 36, München: J. F. Lehmann, 1905.
————. "Theodor Meynert, seine Person, sein Wirken, und sein Werk." *Journal of Psychiatry and Neurology* 40 (1930), 256f.
Benedikt, Moritz. *Aus meinem Leben. Erinnerungen und Erörterungen.* Wien: Verlagsbuchhandlung Carl Konegen, 1906.
Brücke, Ernst Theodor. *Ernst Brücke.* Wien: Julius Springer, 1928.
Brücke, Ernst Wilhelm von. *Briefe an Emil Du Bois-Reymond.* Ed. Hans Brücke. 2 vols. Graz: Akademie Druck- und Verlagsanstalt, 1978.
————. *Bruchstücke aus der Theorie der bildenden Künste.* Leipzig: Brockhaus, 1877.
————. *Schönheit und Fehler der menschlichen Gestalt.* Wien: Braumüller, 1891.
Freud, Ernst, ed. *The Letters of Sigmund Freud.* Trans. Tania and James Stern. New York: Basic Books, 1975.
Freud, Sigmund. *An Autobiographical Study.* Trans. James Strachey. New York: Norton, 1963.
————. *Beyond the Pleasure Principle.* Trans. James Strachey. New York: Norton, 1961.
————. *Civilization and Its Discontents.* Trans. James Strachey. New York: Norton, 1962.
————. *The Ego and the Id.* Trans. Joan Riviere. New York: Norton, 1962.
————. *Die Frage der Laienanalyse.* In his *Gesammelte Werke.* London: Imago, 1948–1955. Vol. 14.
————. *The Future of an Illusion.* Trans. W. D. Robson-Scott. Garden City, N.Y.: Doubleday, 1964.
————. *A General Introduction to Psychoanalysis (Introductory Lectures on Psychoanalysis).* Trans. Joan Riviere. New York: Washington Square Press, 1960.
————. *Group Psychology and the Analysis of the Ego.* Trans. James Strachey. New York: Norton, 1959.

Freud, Sigmund. *The History of the Psychoanalytic Movement.* In *The Basic Writings of Sigmund Freud.* Ed. and trans. A. A. Brill. New York: Modern Library, 1938, pp. 930–980.

———. *Das Ich und das Es.* in his *Gesammelte Werke.* London: Imago, 1948–1955. Vol. 13.

———. *Jenseits des Lustprinzips.* In his *Gesammelte Werke.* London: Imago, 1948–1955. Vol. 13.

———. *Kulturtheoretische Schriften.* Ed. Alexander Mitscherlich, et al. (nine texts on war, religion, and morality). Frankfurt am Main: Fischer, 1986.

———. *Moses and Monotheism.* Trans. Katherine Jones. New York: Vintage, 1967.

———. "The Question of Lay-Analysis." In *Two Short Accounts of Psychoanalysis.* Trans. James Strachey. Middlesex: Penguin, 1966.

———. "The Question of Weltanschauung." In *New Lectures on Psychoanalysis.* New York: Norton, 1965, pp. 158–182.

———. *Totem and Taboo.* In *The Basic Writings of Sigmund Freud.* Ed. and trans. A. A. Brill. New York: Modern Library, 1938, pp. 806–884.

Gupta, R. K. "Freud and Schopenhauer." In *Schopenhauer. His Philosophical Achievement.* Ed. Michael Fox. Totowa, N.J.: Barnes and Noble, 1980, pp. 226–235.

Haeckel, Ernst. "Ein Brief Ernst Haeckels an seine Eltern." In *Ernst Wilhelm von Brücke Briefe an Emil Du Bois-Reymond.* Ed. Hans Brücke. Graz: Akademie Druck- und Verlagsanstalt, 1978, vol. 2, pp. 129–135.

Hartmann, F. "Gedichte von Theodor Meynert." *Wiener klinische Wochenschrift* 18, no. 29 (1905), 5–6.

Hasse, K. E. *Erinnerungen aus meinem Leben.* 2nd ed. Leipzig: n.p., 1902.

Higgins, Mary, and Chester M. Raphael, eds. *Reich Speaks of Freud.* New York: Farrar, Straus and Giroux, 1967.

Hyrtl, Josef. "Abschiedswort an die in Wien versammelten Naturforscher und Ärzte im Jahre 1856." Wien: M. Auer, 1856.

———. "Die materialistische Weltanschauung unserer Zeit." Graz:

Ulrich Mosers Buchhandlung, 1921.

Körner, Josef. *Arthur Schnitzler. Gestalten und Probleme.* Zürich: n.p., 1921.

Kussmaul, A. *Jugenderinnerungen eines alten Arztes.* Stuttgart: n.p., 1899.

Lindken, Hans-Ulrich, ed. *Arthur Schnitzler. Aspekte und Akzente. Materialen zu Leben und Werk.* Frankfurt am Main: Lang, 1984.

Lorenz, Adolf. *My Life and Work. The Search for a Missing Glove.* New York: Scribner, 1936.

Mann, Thomas. "Freud and the Future." In his *Essays.* New York: Vintage, 1958, pp. 303–324.

Masson, Jeffrey, trans and ed. *The Complete Letters of Sigmund Freud to Wilhelm Fliess, 1887–1904.* Cambridge, MA.: Harvard University Press, 1985.

Meynert, Theodor. "Die Bedeutung des Gehirns für das Vorstellungsleben." In his *Sammlung von populär-wissenschaftlichen Vorträgen über den Bau und die Leistungen des Gehirns.* Wien: Braumüller, 1892, pp. 3–16.

———. *Gedichte.* Wien: Braumüller, 1905.

———. "Gehirn und Gesittung." In his *Sammlung,* pp. 139–179.

———. "Karl Rokitansky. Ein Nachruf." In his *Sammlung,* pp. 69–72.

———. "Über den Wahn." In his *Sammlung,* pp. 83–98.

———. "Über die Gefühle." In his *Sammlung,* pp. 42–67.

———. "Über künstliche Störungen des psychischen Gleichgewichts." In his *Sammlung,* pp. 233–253.

Oppolzer, Johann Ritter von. "Über Lehr- und Lernfreiheit." *Wiener medizinische Wochenschrift* 11, no. 3 (1861), 43f. Rpt. TS at the Institut für Geschichte der Medizin, University of Vienna, Abschrift 53.

Puschmann, Theodor. *Die Medicin in Wien während der letzten 100 Jahre.* Wien: Perles, 1884.

Reik, Theodor. *From Thirty Years with Freud.* New York: Farrar and Rinehart, 1940.

Rieff, Philip, ed. *Character and Culture.* Twenty-eight essays by

Sigmund Freud. New York: Collier, 1963.

Rokitansky, Karl. "Der selbstständige Werth des Wissens." Wien: K. und K. Hof- und Staatsdruckerei, 1867.

———. "Die Solidarität alles Thierlebens." Wien: K. und K. Hof- und Staatsdruckerei, 1869.

Scheible, Hartmut, ed. *Arthur Schnitzler in Selbstzeugnissen und Bilddokumenten.* Reinbek bei Hamburg: Rowohlt, 1976.

Schnitzler, Arthur. *Aphorismen und Betrachtungen.* Ed. Robert O. Weiss. Frankfurt am Main: Fischer, 1967.

———. *Briefe 1875–1912.* Eds. Therese Nickl and Heinrich Schnitzler. Frankfurt am Main: Fischer, 1981.

———. *Briefe 1913–1931.* Eds. Peter Braunwarth, et al. Frankfurt am Main: Fischer, 1984.

———. "Casanovas Heimfahrt." In his *Das erzählerische Werk.* Frankfurt am Main: Fischer, 1985, vol. 5.

———. "Doktor Gräsler, Badearzt." In his *Das erzählerische Werk.* Frankfurt am Main: Fischer, 1984, vol. 3.

———. "Flucht in die Finsternis." In his *Das erzählerische Werk.* Frankfurt am Main: Fischer, 1984, vol. 5.

———. "Frau Beate und ihr Sohn." In his *Das erzählerische Werk.* Frankfurt am Main: Fischer, 1984, vol. 3.

———. "Fräulein Else." In his *Das erzählerische Werk.* Frankfurt am Main: Fischer, 1984, vol. 5.

———. *Der Gang zum Weiher.* In his *Das dramatische Werk.* Frankfurt am Main: Fischer, 1984, vol. 8.

———. *Der Geist im Wort und der Geist in der Tat. Vorläufige Bemerkungen zu zwei Diagrammen.* Berlin: Fischer, 1927.

———. *Jugend in Wien. Eine Autobiographie.* Frankfurt am Main: Fischer, 1981.

———. *My Youth in Vienna.* Trans. Catherine Hutter. New York: Holt, Rinehart and Winston, 1970.

———. *Professor Bernhardi.* In his *Das dramatische Werk.* Frankfurt am Main: Fischer, 1984, vol. 6.

———. Review of Theodor Meynert's *Klinische Vorlesungen über Psychiatrie. Internationale klinische Rundschau* 5 (1891), 162.

———. Review of Theodor Meynert's *Sammlung. Internationale klinische Rundschau* 6 (1892), 778–779.

———. "Der Sohn. Aus den Papieren eines Arztes." In his *Das erzählerische Werk*. Frankfurt am Main: Fischer, 1977, vol. 1.

———. "Spiel im Morgengrauen." In his *Das erzählerische Werk*. Frankfurt am Main: Fischer, 1984, vol. 6.

———. *Therese*. In his *Das erzählerische Werk*. Frankfurt am Main: Fischer, 1984, vol. 7.

———. "Traumnovelle." In his *Das erzählerische Werk*. Frankfurt am Main: Fischer, 1984, vol. 6.

———. *Über Krieg und Frieden*. Stockholm: Bermann-Fischer, 1939.

———. *Der Weg ins Freie*. In his *Das erzählerische Werk*. Frankfurt am Main: Fischer, 1984, vol. 4.

Schnitzler, Heinrich, et al., eds. *Arthur Schnitzler. Sein Leben, sein Werk, seine Zeit*. Frankfurt am Main: Fischer, 1981.

———. ed. "Briefe Sigmund Freuds an Arthur Schnitzler." *Die neue Rundschau* 46 (1955), 95–106.

Schnitzler, Olga. *Spiegelbild der Freundschaft*. Salzburg: Residenz, 1962.

Sterba, Richard F. *Reminiscences of a Viennese Psychoanalyst*. Detroit: Wayne State University Press, 1982.

Stockert-Meynert, Dora. *Theodor Meynert und seine Zeit. Zur Geistesgeschichte Österreichs in der zweiten Hälfte des neunzehnten Jahrhunderts*. Wien: Österreichischer Bundesverlag, 1930.

Urbach, Reinhard, ed. *Arthur Schnitzler. Entworfenes und Verworfenes. Aus dem Nachlaß*. Frankfurt am Main: Fischer, 1977.

———. ed. "Arthur Schnitzler über Psychoanalyse." *Protokolle* 2 (1976), 277–284.

Urban, Bernd, ed. "Vier unveröffentlichte Briefe Arthur Schnitzlers an den Psychoanalytiker Theodor Reik." *Modern Austrian Literature* 8, no. 3/4 (1975), 236–247.

Wagner-Jauregg, Julius. "Josef Skoda und Theodor Meynert."

Wiener medizinische Wochenschrift no. 2, 1927, pp. 4–9.
———. *Lebenserinnerungen.* Eds. L. Schönbauer and M. Jantsch. Wien: Amalthea, 1950.

Wittels, Fritz. *Sigmund Freud: His Personality, His Teaching and His School.* New York: Dodd, Mead, 1924.

Wortis, Joseph. *Fragments of an Analysis with Freud.* New York: Simon and Schuster, 1954.

Zuckerkandl, Bertha. *Österreich Intim. Erinnerungen 1892–1942.* Wien: Amalthea, 1981.

Zweig, Stefan. *Die Welt von Gestern. Erinnerungen eines Europäers.* Stockholm: Bermann-Fischer, 1944.

III. Secondary Sources

A. Unpublished

Johnston, William M. "Die Wiener Aphoristiker und Karl Kraus." Karl Kraus Symposium May 12–May 16, 1986, Palais Palffy, Vienna, May 12, 1986.

Leser, Norbert. "The Intellectual Life of Vienna during the Inter-War Period." Brandeis University, March 21, 1983.

Lesky, Erna. "Pathology and Internal Medicine during the Positivistic World in Austria (1836–1914)." TS (German) at the Institut für Geschichte der Medizin, University of Vienna, no. 42.772.

Leupold-Löwenthal, Harald. "A Viennese in Paris – Sigmund Freud: Paris 1885/86." Institut Français, Vienna, January 23, 1986.

Miciotto, Robert J. "Carl Rokitansky: Nineteenth-Century Pathologist and Leader of the New Vienna School." Diss. Johns Hopkins University, 1979.

B. Published

Abels, Norbert. *Sicherheit ist nirgends. Judentum und Aufklärung bei Arthur Schnitzler.* Königstein/Ts.: Anton Hain Messenheim, 1982.

Alter, Marie P. "Schnitzler's Physician: An Existentialist Character." *Modern Austrian Literature* 4, no. 3 (Fall 1971), 7–23.

Amacher, Peter. *Freud's Neurological Education and Its Influence on Psychoanalytic Theory.* New York: International Universities Press, 1965.

Arens, Detlev. *Untersuchungen zu Arthur Schnitzlers Roman "Der Weg ins Freie."* Frankfurt am Main: Peter Lang, 1981.

Aspetsberger, Friedbert. "Arthur Schnitzlers *Der Weg ins Freie. Sprachkunst. Beiträge zur Literaturwissenschaft* 4, Heft 1/2 (1973), 65–80.

Bailey, Percival. *Sigmund the Unserene, A Tragedy in Three Acts.* Springfield, Illinois: Charles Thomas, 1965.

Bakan, David. *Sigmund Freud and the Jewish Mystical Tradition.* Princeton, New Jersey: Van Nostrand, 1958.

Barea, Ilsa. *Vienna.* New York: Knopf, 1966.

Bareikis, Robert. "Arthur Schnitzler's 'Fräulein Else': A Freudian Novella?" *Literature and Psychology* 19 (1969), 19–32.

Baumann, Gerhart. *Arthur Schnitzler. Die Welt von Gestern eines Dichters von Morgen.* Bonn: Athenäum, 1965.

Beharriell, Frederick J. "Arthur Schnitzler's Range of Theme." *Monatshefte* 43 (1951), 301–311.

———. "Freud's 'Double': Arthur Schnitzler." *Journal of the American Psychoanalytic Association* 10 (1962), 722–730.

Berlin, Jeffrey B. "Political Criticism in Arthur Schnitzler's *Aphorismen und Betrachtungen.*" *Neophilologus* 57 (1973), 173–178.

Bernfeld, Siegfried. "Freud's Earliest Theories and the School of Helmholtz." *Psychoanalytic Quarterly* 13, no. 3 (1944), 341–362.

———. "Freud's Scientific Beginnings." *American Imago* 6 (1949), 165–196.

———. "Sigmund Freud, MD." *International Journal of Psychoanalysis* 32 (1951), 204–217.

Bettelheim, Bruno. *Freud and Man's Soul.* New York: Vintage, 1984.

Borges, Jorge Luis. "The Double." In his *The Book of Imaginary Beings.* New York: Dutton, 1970, pp. 80–81.

Brandell, Gunnar, *Freud: A Man of His Century.* Sussex: Harvester, 1979.

Broch, Hermann. "Hofmannsthal und seine Zeit." In his *Dichten und Erkennen. Essays.* Zürich: Rhein, 1955, vol. 1, pp. 43–182.

Brome, Vincent. *Freud and His Early Circle: The Struggles of Psychoanalysis.* London: William Heinemann, 1967.

Bry, Else, and Alfred H. Rifkin. "Freud and the History of Ideas: Primary Sources 1886–1910." *Science and Psychoanalysis* 5 (1962), 6–36.

Buess, Heinrich. "Zur Frage des therapeutischen Nihilismus im neunzehnten Jahrhundert." *Schweizer medizinische Wochenschrift* 87 (1957), Beiheft zur no. 14, pp. 444–447.

Clark, Ronald. *Freud: The Man and the Cause.* New York: Random House, 1980.

Couch, Lotte S. "Der Reigen: Arthur Schnitzler und Sigmund Freud." *Österreich in Geschichte und Literatur* 16 (1972), 217–227.

Decker, Hannah S. "Conclusion: Idealism and Positivism." In her *Freud in Germany: Revolution and Reaction in Science, 1893–1907.* Psychological Issues, Monograph 41. New York: International Universities Press, 1977, pp. 321–329.

De Crinis, M. "Meynert in seinem Eindruck auf die moderne psychiatrische Forschung." *Wiener klinische Wochenschrift,* Separatabdruck, July 20, 1942, Article 907.

Dilman, Ilham. *Freud and Human Nature.* Oxford: Basil Blackwell, 1983.

Dorer, Maria. *Historische Grundlagen der Psychoanalyse.* Leipzig: n.p., 1932.

Drucker, Peter. "Freudian Myths and Freudian Realities." In his *Adventures of a Bystander.* New York: Harper and Row, 1979, pp. 83-99.

Eckert, Willehad Paul. "Arthur Schnitzler und das Wiener Judentum." *EMUNA Horizonte zur Diskussion über Israel und das Judentum* 8, no. 2 (März/April, 1973), 118–130.

Eissler, Kurt R. "Psychoanalytische Einfälle zu Freuds 'Zerstreute(n) Gedanken.'" In Eissler, et al. *Aus Freuds Sprachwelt und andere Beiträge.* Bern: Hans Huber, 1974, pp. 104–127.

Ellenberger, Henri. "Sigmund Freud and Psychoanalysis." In his *The Discovery of the Unconscious: The History and Evolution of Dynamic Psychiatry.* New York: Basic Books, 1970, Chapter Seven, pp. 418–570.

Esslin, Martin. "Freud's Vienna." In Jonathan Miller, ed., *Freud: The Man, His World, His Influence.* Boston: Little, Brown, 1972, pp. 42–54.

Farley, Timothy. "Arthur Schnitzler's Sociopolitical Märchen." In Petrus W. Tax and Richard H. Lawson, eds. *Arthur Schnitzler and His Age: Intellectual and Artistic Currents.* Bonn: Bouvier, 1984, pp. 104–119.

Fromm, Erich. *The Anatomy of Human Destructiveness.* New York: Fawcett Crest, 1973.

———. *Greatness and Limitations of Freud's Thought.* New York: Harper and Row, 1980.

———. *Sigmund Freud's Mission.* New York: Grove Press, 1959.

Fuchs, Albert. *Geistige Strömungen in Österreich 1867–1918.* Wien: Globus, 1949.

Garnham, Sarah. *The Habsburg Twilight: Tales from Vienna.* New York: Atheneum, 1979.

Gay, Peter. *Freud, Jews and Other Germans: Masters and Victims in Modernist Culture.* Oxford: Oxford University Press, 1978.

———. *A Godless Jew: Freud, Atheism, and the Making of Psychoanalysis.* New Haven: Yale University Press, 1987.

Geha, Richard E. "Freud as Fictionalist: The Imaginary Worlds of Psychoanalysis." In *Freud: Appraisals and Reappraisals,* vol. 2, ed. Paul E. Stepansky. Hillsdale, New Jersey: The Analytic Press, 1988.

Grollman, Earl A. *Judaism in Sigmund Freud's World.* New York: Appleton-Century-Crofts, 1965.

Hausner, Harry H. "Die Beziehungen zwischen Arthur Schnitzler und Sigmund Freud." *Modern Austrian Literature* 3, no. 2 (1970), 48–61.

Heer, Friedrich. "Freud, the Viennese Jew." In Jonathan Miller, ed. *Freud: The Man, His World, His Influence.* Boston: Little, Brown, 1972, pp. 1–20.

—— *Der Kampf um die österreichische Identität.* Wien: Böhlau, 1981.

Heller, Peter. "Freud as a Phenomenon of the Fin de Siècle." In Tax and Lawson, eds. *Arthur Schnitzler and His Age: Intellectual and Artistic Currents,* pp. 2–28.

Hermann, Imre. "Goethes Aufsatz 'Die Natur' und Freuds weitere philosophisch-psychologische Lektüre aus den Jahren 1880–1900." *Jahrbuch der Psychoanalyse* 7 (1974), 77–100.

Herzog, Patricia. "The Myth of Freud as Anti-Philosopher." In *Freud: Appraisals and Reappraisals,* vol. 2, ed. Paul E. Stepansky. Hillsdale, New Jersey: The Analytic Press, 1988.

Holt, Robert R. "Freud's Adolescent Reading: Some Possible Effects on His Work." In *Freud: Appraisals and Reappraisals,* vol. 3, ed. Paul E. Stepansky. Hillsdale, New Jersey: The Analytic Press, 1988.

Horkheimer, Max, and Theodor W. Adorno. *Dialectic of Enlightenment.* New York: Herder and Herder, 1972.

Hughes, H. Stuart. *Consciousness and Society: The Reorientation of European Thought.* New York: Vintage, 1977.

Husteda, Franz. "Du Bois-Reymond, Emil." *Encyclopedia of Philosophy.* 1972 edition.

Isbister, J. N. *Freud: An Introduction to His Life and Work.* Cambridge: Polity Press, 1985.

Janik, Allan, and Stephan Toulmin. *Wittgenstein's Vienna.* New York: Simon and Schuster, 1973.

Johnston, William M. *The Austrian Mind: An Intellectual and Social History 1848–1938.* Berkeley: University of California Press, 1972.

Jones, Ernest. *Sigmund Freud: Life and Work.* 3 vols. London:

Hogarth, 1953–1957.

Just, Gottfried. *Ironie und Sentimentalität in den erzählenden Dichtungen Arthur Schnitzlers.* Berlin: Erich Schmidt, 1968.

Kann, Robert A. "The Image of the Austrian in the Writings of Arthur Schnitzler." In Herbert Reichert and Herman Salinger, eds. *Studies in Arthur Schnitzler.* Chapel Hill: University of North Carolina Press, 1963, pp. 45–70.

Kanzer, Mark. "Freud and His Literary Doubles." *American Imago* 33 (1976), 231–243.

Kerr, John. "Beyond the Pleasure Principle and Back Again: Freud, Jung, and Sabina Spielrein." In *Freud: Appraisals and Reappraisals,* vol. 3, ed. Paul E. Stepansky. Hillsdale, New Jersey: The Analytic Press, 1988.

Kohn, Hans. *Karl Kraus, Arthur Schnitzler, Otto Weininger. Aus dem jüdischen Wien der Jahrhundertwende.* Tübingen: J.C.B. Mohr, 1962.

Kupper, Herbert I., and Hilda S. Rollman-Branch. "Freud and Schnitzler (Doppelgänger)." *Journal of the American Psychoanalytic Association* 7 (1959), 109–126.

Lawson Richard H. "Thematic Reflections of the 'Song of Love and Play and Death' in Schnitzler's Fiction." In Tax and Lawson, eds., *Arthur Schnitzler and His Age,* pp. 70–89.

Lebzeltern, Gustav. "Sigmund Freud and Theodor Meynert." *Wiener klinische Wochenschrift* 85 (1973), 417–422.

Lederer, Herbert. "Arthur Schnitzler before *Anatol.*" *Germanic Review* 36 (1961), 269–281.

Leibbrand, Werner. "Karl von Rokitansky und Schopenhauer." In *35. Schopenhauer Jahrbuch für die Jahre 1953–1954,* pp. 75–77.

Leitner, Helmut. "Straßennamen – Zeugen berühmter Ärzte: Johann Ritter von Oppolzer." *Arzt Presse Medizin* 34,. no. 7 (September 1978), 4–7.

Lesky, Erna. "Carl von Rokitansky." In *Große Österreicher* vol. 12. Zürich, 1957, pp. 38–51.

———. "Josef Skoda." *Wiener klinische Wochenschrift* 68 (1956),

726–729.

———. *The Vienna Medical School in the Nineteenth Century.* Baltimore: Johns Hopkins University Press, 1976.

———. "Von den Ursprüngen des therapeutischen Nihilismus." *Sudhoffs Archiv für Geschichte der Medizin und der Naturwissenschaften* 44 (1960), 1–20.

———. "Wien 1879–Medizinisches Porträt der Metropole." *Wiener klinische Wochenschrift* 63 (1951), Separatabdruck, Jg. 129, no. 6 (1979), 152–156.

Löffler, Wilhelm. "Skoda im Wendepunkt der Medizin." *Wiener klinische Wochenschrift* 63 (1951), 618f, 771f.

Ludwig, Emil. *Doctor Freud.* New York: Manor Books, 1949.

Lyons, Albert S., and Joseph R. Petrucelli. *Medicine. An Illustrated History.* New York: Harry N. Abrams, 1978.

Magris, Claudio. "Arthur Schnitzler und das Karussell der Triebe." In Hartmut Scheible, ed. *Arthur Schnitzler in neuer Sicht.* München: Fink, 1981, pp. 71–80.

Marcuse, Herbert. *Eros and Civilization: A Philosophical Inquiry into Freud.* New York: Vintage, 1955.

Marcuse, Ludwig. *Sigmund Freud. Sein Bild von Menschen.* Hamburg: n.p., 1956.

McGrath, William J. *Freud's Discovery of Psychoanalysis: The Politics of Hysteria.* Ithaca, New York: Cornell University Press, 1986.

Nehring, Wolfgang. "Schnitzler, Freud's Alter Ego?" *Modern Austrian Literature* 10, nos. 3/4 (1977), 179–194.

Neuburger, Max. *Die Entwicklung der Medizin in Österreich.* Wien: Carl Fromme, 1918.

———. "Rokitansky als Vorkämpfer der mechanistischen Forschungsmethode und der idealistischen Weltanschauung." *Wiener klinische Wochenschrift,* Sonderabdruck, no. 12 (1934).

Oswald, Victor A., Jr., and Veronica Pinter Mindess. "Schnitzler's 'Fräulein Else' and the Psychoanalytic Theory of Neuroses." *Germanic Review* 26 (1951), 279–288.

Paal, Janos. "Freuds Verhältnis zum Judentum." *EMUNA Hori-*

zonte zur Diskussion über Israel und das Judentum 8, no. 2, (März/April 1973), 136–140.

Politzer, Heinz. "Diagnose und Dichtung. Zum Werk Arthur Schnitzlers." In *Das Schweigen der Sirenen. Studien zur deutschen und österreichischen Literatur.* Stuttgart: Metzler, 1968, pp. 110–141.

Rella, Franco. "Freud und Schnitzler. Der Spiegel der Analyse." In *Arthur Schnitzler in neuer Sicht.* Ed. Hartmut Scheible. München: Fink, 1981, pp. 200–206.

Rey, William H. *Arthur Schnitzler. Die späte Prosa als Gipfel seines Schaffens.* Berlin: Schmidt, 1968.

———. *Arthur Schnitzler. Professor Bernhardi.* München: Fink, 1971.

Rieff, Philip. *Freud: The Mind of the Moralist.* Garden City, New York: Doubleday, 1961.

Riese, Walter. "The Impact of Nineteenth Century Thought on Psychiatry." *International Record of Medicine* 173 (January 1960), 7–19.

———. "An Outline of a History of Ideas in Psychotherapy." *Bulletin of the History of Medicine* 25 (1951), 442–456.

———. "The Pre-Freudian Origins of Psychoanalysis." In *Science and Psychoanalysis,* vol. 1, ed. Jules H. Massermann. New York: Gruen and Stratton, 1958, pp. 23–72.

Roazen, Paul. *Freud and His Followers.* London: Penguin, 1974.

———. *Freud: Political and Social Thought.* New York: Vintage, 1971.

Robert, Marthe. *Die Revolution der Psychoanalyse. Leben und Werk von Sigmund Freud.* Frankfurt am Main: Fischer, 1967.

———. *Sigmund Freud. Zwischen Moses und Oedipus.* München: List, 1975.

Rosen, George. "Freud and Medicine in Vienna." In Jonathan Miller, ed. *Freud,* pp. 1–20.

Rothschuh, Karl. "Hyrtl contra Brücke. Ein Gelehrtenstreit im 19. Jahrhundert und seine Hintergründe." *Clio Medica* 9, no. 2 (1974), 81–92.

Rozenblit, Marsha C. *The Jews of Vienna: Assimilation and Identity, 1867-1914*. New York: State University of New York Press, 1984.

Rubenstein, Richard L. "Freud and Judaism: A Review Article." *Journal of Religion* 47 (1967), 39–44.

———. "The Unmastered Trauma: The Elimination of the European Jews." In his *The Age of Triage. Fear and Hope in an Overcrowded World*. Boston: Beacon, 1983, pp. 128–164.

Scheible, Hartmut. "Arthur Schnitzler. Figur, Situation, Gestalt." In his *Arthur Schnitzler in neuer Sicht*. München: Fink, 1981, pp. 12–33.

———. *Arthur Schnitzler und die Aufklärung*. München: Fink, 1971.

———. *Literarischer Jugendstil in Wien*. München: Artemis, 1984.

Scheuzger, Jürg. *Das Spiel mit Typen und Typenkonstellationen in den Dramen Arthur Schnitzlers*. Zürich: Juris Druck, 1975.

Schlein, Rena R. "Arthur Schnitzler: Author-Scientist." *Modern Austrian Literature* 11, no. 2 (Summer 1968), 28–38.

Schnitzler, Heinrich. "Gay Vienna—Myth and Reality." *Journal of the History of Ideas* 15 (1954), 94–118.

Schorske, Carl E. *Fin-de-Siècle Vienna: Politics and Culture*. New York: Knopf, 1980.

Schröter, Klaus. "Maximen und Reflexionen des jungen Freud." In *Aus Freuds Sprachwelt und andere Beiträge*. Bern: n.p., 1974, pp. 129–186.

Schur, Max. *Freud: Living and Dying*. New York: International Universities Press, 1972.

Sigerist, H. E. "Carl Rokitansky." In *Große Ärzte*. 4th ed. München: n.p., 1959, pp. 260–272.

Silverstein, Barry. " 'Now Comes a Sad Story': Freud's Lost Metapsychological Papers." In *Freud: Appraisals and Reappraisals*, vol. 1, ed. Paul E. Stepansky. Hillsdale, New Jersey: The Analytic Press, 1986.

Spector, Jack J. *The Aesthetics of Freud: A Study in Psycho-*

164   Mark Luprecht

analysis and Art. New York: Praeger, 1972.

Stepansky, Paul E. *A History of Aggression in Freud.* Psychological Issues, Monograph 39. New York: International Universities Press, 1977.

Sternberg, Maximilian. *Josef Skoda.* Wien: Springer, 1924.

Sulloway, Frank J. *Freud. The Biologist of the Mind.* New York: Basic Books, 1979.

Swales, Martin. *Arthur Schnitzler. A Critical Study.* Oxford: Clarendon, 1971.

Swales, Peter J. "Freud, His Teacher, and the Birth of Psychoanalysis." In *Freud: Appraisals and Reappraisals,* vol. 1, ed. Paul E. Stepansky. Hillsdale, New Jersey: The Analytic Press, 1986.

Török, Andrew. "Arthur Schnitzler's *Der Weg ins Freie.* Versuch einer Neuinterpretation." *Monatshefte* 64 (Winter 1972), 371–377.

Trosman, Harry. *Freud and the Imaginative World.* Hillsdale, New Jersey: The Analytic Press, 1985.

Urbach, Reinhard. *Arthur Schnitzler.* New York: Ungar, 1973.

Urban, Bernd. "Arthur Schnitzler und Sigmund Freud. Aus den Anfängen des 'Doppelgängers.' Zur Differenzierung dichterischer Intuition und Umgebung der frühen Hysterieforschung." *Germanisch-Romanisch Monatsschrift* 24 (1974), 193–223.

Vogl, Alfred. "Six Hundred Years of Medicine in Vienna." In *Essays on the History of Medicine.* New York: Neale Watson Academic Publishers, 1976, pp. 309–326.

Wagner, Renate. *Arthur Schnitzler. Eine Biographie.* Wien: Molden, 1981.

Wallace, Edwin R., IV. "Freud as Ethicist." In *Freud: Appraisals and Reappraisals,* vol. 1, ed. Paul E. Stepansky. Hillsdale, New Jersey: The Analytic Press, 1986.

———. "The Place of *Totem and Taboo* in Freud's Subsequent Socio-Cultural Thinking." In his *Freud and Anthropology: A History and Reappraisal.* Psychological Issues Monograph 55. New York: International Universities Press,

1983, pp. 248–259.

Weiss, Robert O. "The Human Element in Arthur Schnitzler's Social Criticism." *Modern Austrian Literature* 5, nos. 1/2 (1972), 30–44.

———. "The Psychoses in the Works of Arthur Schnitzler." *German Quarterly* 41 (1968), 377–400.

———. "A Study of the Psychiatric Elements in Schnitzler's 'Flucht in die Finsternis.'" *Germanic Review* 33 (1958), 189–275.

Worbs, Michael. *Nervenkunst. Literatur und Psychoanalyse im Wien der Jahrhundertwende.* Frankfurt am Main: Europäische Verlagsanstalt, 1983.

Zohn, Harry. "Arthur Schnitzler und das Judentum." In his *Wiener Juden in der deutschen Literatur.* Tel Aviv: Olamenu, 1964, pp. 9–18.

NAME INDEX

172